ISBN 978-1-332-25213-8
PIBN 10304588

1 MONTH OF
FREE
READING

at

www.ForgottenBooks.com

By purchasing this book you are eligible for one month membership to ForgottenBooks.com, giving you unlimited access to our entire collection of over 1,000,000 titles via our web site and mobile apps.

To claim your free month visit:

www.forgottenbooks.com/free304588

English
Français
Deutsche
Italiano
Español
Português

www.forgottenbooks.com

Mythology Photography **Fiction**
Fishing Christianity **Art** Cooking
Essays Buddhism Freemasonry
Medicine **Biology** Music **Ancient
Egypt** Evolution Carpentry Physics
Dance Geology **Mathematics** Fitness
Shakespeare **Folklore** Yoga Marketing
Confidence Immortality Biographies
Poetry **Psychology** Witchcraft
Electronics Chemistry History **Law**
Accounting **Philosophy** Anthropology
Alchemy Drama Quantum Mechanics
Atheism Sexual Health **Ancient History**
Entrepreneurship Languages Sport
Paleontology Needlework Islam
Metaphysics Investment Archaeology
Parenting Statistics Criminology
Motivational

ARE EXISTING PRIVATE SECTOR AND STATE-OPERATED HEALTH CARE ALLIANCES WORKING?

Y 4. G 74/7: H 34/21

Are Existing Private Sector and Sta...

HEARING

BEFORE THE

HUMAN RESOURCES AND INTERGOVERNMENTAL RELATIONS SUBCOMMITTEE

OF THE

COMMITTEE ON GOVERNMENT OPERATIONS HOUSE OF REPRESENTATIVES

ONE HUNDRED THIRD CONGRESS

SECOND SESSION

JUNE 30, 1994

Printed for the use of the Committee on Government Operations

U.S. GOVERNMENT PRINTING OFFICE

85–738   WASHINGTON : 1997

For sale by the U.S. Government Printing Office
Superintendent of Documents, Congressional Sales Office, Washington, DC 20402
ISBN 0-16-055507-8

ARE EXISTING PRIVATE SECTOR AND STATE-OPERATED HEALTH CARE ALLIANCES WORKING?

Y 4. G 74/7: H 34/21

Are Existing Private Sector and Sta...

HEARING

BEFORE THE

HUMAN RESOURCES AND INTERGOVERNMENTAL RELATIONS SUBCOMMITTEE

OF THE

COMMITTEE ON GOVERNMENT OPERATIONS HOUSE OF REPRESENTATIVES

ONE HUNDRED THIRD CONGRESS

SECOND SESSION

JUNE 30, 1994

Printed for the use of the Committee on Government Operations

U.S. GOVERNMENT PRINTING OFFICE

85-738

WASHINGTON : 1997

For sale by the U.S. Government Printing Office
Superintendent of Documents, Congressional Sales Office, Washington, DC 20402
ISBN 0-16-055507-8

COMMITTEE ON GOVERNMENT OPERATIONS

JOHN CONYERS, JR., Michigan, *Chairman*

CARDISS COLLINS, Illinois
HENRY A. WAXMAN, California
MIKE SYNAR, Oklahoma
STEPHEN L. NEAL, North Carolina
TOM LANTOS, California
MAJOR R. OWENS, New York
EDOLPHUS TOWNS, New York
JOHN M. SPRATT, JR., South Carolina
GARY A. CONDIT, California
COLLIN C. PETERSON, Minnesota
KAREN L. THURMAN, Florida
BOBBY L. RUSH, Illinois
CAROLYN B. MALONEY, New York
THOMAS M. BARRETT, Wisconsin
DONALD M. PAYNE, New Jersey
FLOYD H. FLAKE, New York
JAMES A. HAYES, Louisiana
CRAIG A. WASHINGTON, Texas
BARBARA-ROSE COLLINS, Michigan
CORRINE BROWN, Florida
MARJORIE MARGOLIES-MEZVINSKY,
   Pennsylvania
LYNN C. WOOLSEY, California
GENE GREEN, Texas
BART STUPAK, Michigan

WILLIAM F. CLINGER, JR., Pennsylvania
AL McCANDLESS, California
J. DENNIS HASTERT, Illinois
JON L. KYL, Arizona
CHRISTOPHER SHAYS, Connecticut
STEVEN SCHIFF, New Mexico
CHRISTOPHER COX, California
CRAIG THOMAS, Wyoming
ILEANA ROS-LEHTINEN, Florida
DICK ZIMMER, New Jersey
WILLIAM H. ZELIFF, JR., New Hampshire
JOHN M. McHUGH, New York
STEPHEN HORN, California
DEBORAH PRYCE, Ohio
JOHN L. MICA, Florida
ROB PORTMAN, Ohio
FRANK D. LUCAS, Oklahoma

BERNARD SANDERS, Vermont
   (Independent)

JULIAN EPSTEIN, *Staff Director*
MATTHEW R. FLETCHER, *Minority Staff Director*

HUMAN RESOURCES AND INTERGOVERNMENTAL RELATIONS SUBCOMMITTEE

EDOLPHUS TOWNS, New York, *Chairman*

HENRY A. WAXMAN, California
THOMAS M. BARRETT, Wisconsin
DONALD M. PAYNE, New Jersey
CRAIG A. WASHINGTON, Texas

STEVEN SCHIFF, New Mexico
JOHN L. MICA, Florida
ROB PORTMAN, Ohio

BERNARD SANDERS, Vermont (Ind.)

EX OFFICIO

JOHN CONYERS, JR., Michigan

WILLIAM F. CLINGER, JR., Pennsylvania

RONALD A. STROMAN, *Staff Director*
MARTINE M. DiCROCE, *Clerk*
MARTHA MORGAN, *Minority Professional Staff Member*

CONTENTS

ARE EXISTING PRIVATE SECTOR AND STATE-OPERATED HEALTH CARE ALLIANCES WORKING?

THURSDAY, JUNE 30, 1994

HOUSE OF REPRESENTATIVES,
SUBCOMMITTEE ON HUMAN RESOURCES
AND INTERGOVERNMENTAL RELATIONS,
COMMITTEE ON GOVERNMENT OPERATIONS,
Washington, DC.

The subcommittee met, pursuant to notice, at 10:08 a.m., in room 2247, Rayburn House Office Building, Hon. Edolphus Towns (chairman of the subcommittee) presiding.

Present: Representatives Towns, Schiff, and Mica.

Staff present: Ronald A. Stroman, staff director; Martine M. DiCroce, clerk; and Martha Morgan, minority professional staff member.

Mr. TOWNS. The Subcommittee on Human Resources and International Relations will come to order.

We have all seen the "Harry and Louise" commercial in which Louise condemns health care purchasing alliances as large, bloated government bureaucracy. This and other scare tactics are, unfortunately, misleading the American people about workable health care reform.

The truth is that numerous States and small businesses all over this country have either created or are considering health care purchasing alliances as part of a local health care reform initiative. Almost every health care proposal currently under consideration by Congress contains some form of voluntary alliance structure as a way to provide affordable health care insurance.

But these alliances are a mystery to most of us. We know little about how health alliances really work. Most people have no idea who will run these alliances. Will we have to go through a maze of bureaucrats in order to see a doctor? How do alliances interact with existing government health care systems like Medicare and Medicaid? Would they really limit our choice of health care plans as we have been told?

In order to get the facts about health care purchasing alliances, this subcommittee asked the General Accounting Office to examine the operation of existing health purchasing alliances in several States: California, Florida, Minnesota, Ohio, Washington, and Wisconsin. We also asked GAO to look at the private sector operations of purchasing alliances.

(1)

Today, we will hear the results of the investigation, and we will hear from some of the people who are responsible for overseeing the operation of these alliances at the local level.

The results of GAO's investigation of alliances are encouraging. GAO has found that existing voluntary alliances are not big bureaucracies. Most alliances operate with small in-house staffs which means lower operating costs.

Public alliances generally offer a large choice of health care plans. For example, State-run alliances in Wisconsin and California each offer over 25 health plans. Interestingly, it is the private sector alliances which tend to limit the choice of health plans.

The GAO report does, however, raise an area of deep concern to me regarding the composition of the boards which operate these alliances. I believe that membership of an alliance should be fairly balanced to represent the interests of senior citizens, businesses, minorities and consumers.

The report suggests that a reasonable balance has not occurred voluntarily within public or private sector alliances. Without this balance, I fear that major segments of our society will not participate in the alliances because of a lack of confidence in the ability of alliances to fairly represent them.

This would be unfortunate, since we would lose a major tool in our efforts to provide affordable and quality health care for all Americans.

At this time I would like to yield for an opening statement to Congressman Schiff from Albuquerque, NM.

[The prepared statement of Hon. Edolphus Towns follows:]

OPENING STATEMENT CHAIRMAN EDOLPHUS TOWNS
SUBCOMMITTEE ON HUMAN RESOURCES AND
INTERGOVERNMENTAL RELATIONS
GOVERNMENT OPERATIONS COMMITTEE

JUNE 30, 1994

We have all seen the Harry and Louise commercial in which Louise condemns health care purchasing alliances as large bloated government bureaucracies. This and other scare tactics, are unfortunately, misleading the American people about workable health care reform.

The truth is that numerous states and small businesses all over this country have either created or are considering health care purchasing alliances as part of local health care reform initiatives. Almost every health care proposal currently under consideration by Congress contains some form of voluntary alliance structure as a way to provide affordable health care insurance. But these alliances are a mystery to most of us.

We know little about how health alliances really work. Most people have no idea who will run these alliances. Will we have to go through a maze of government bureaucrats in order to see a doctor? How do alliances interact with existing government health care systems like Medicare and Medicaid? Will they really limit our choice of health care plans as we have been told?

In order to get the facts about health care purchasing alliances, this Subcommittee asked the General Accounting Office to examine the operation of existing health purchasing alliances in California, Florida, Minnesota, Ohio, Washington, and Wisconsin. We also asked GAO to look at the private sector's operation of purchasing alliances. Today we will hear the results of that investigation, and we will hear from some of the people who are responsible for overseeing the operation of these alliances at the local level.

The results of GAO's investigation of alliances are encouraging. GAO has found that existing voluntary alliances are not big bureaucracies. Most alliances operate with small in-house staffs, which means lower operating costs.

Public alliances generally offer a large choice of health plans. For example, state-run alliances in Wisconsin and California each offer over 25 health plans. Interestingly, it is the private sector alliances which tend to limit the choices of health plans.

The GAO report does however, raise an area of deep concern to me regarding the composition of the boards which operate these alliances. I believe that membership of alliance boards should be fairly balanced to represent the interests of senior citizens, businesses, minorities and consumers. This report suggests that a reasonable balance has not occurred voluntarily within public or private sector alliances. Without this balance, I fear that major segments of our society will not participate in the alliances structure because of a lack of confidence in the ability of alliances to fairly represent them. This would be unfortunate, since we would lose a major tool in our effort to provide affordable and quality health care for all Americans.

Mr. SCHIFF. Thank you, Mr. Chairman. I will be brief.

First I want to thank you and commend you for holding this hearing. Once again you have selected a subject which is in the forefront of the health care debate and making a contribution to that debate.

Second of all, I have to distinguish between the idea, at least as I see it, of regional health care alliances and the Clinton administration original health care proposal. I think that there is a major difference between the two.

It is true, of course, that the original Clinton plan is set up on the idea of regional alliances. But the difference is that under the Clinton plan, with only a few exceptions, everyone in the United States is compelled to join the government-run health care alliance whether they want to or not. Even people who are totally satisfied with their present health care are required under that proposed law to give up what they have and to join a health care alliance. And for myself, that is the main objection to health care alliances as advanced by the Clinton administration.

But the idea of a health care alliance in itself, the idea of coalescing individuals, and small businesses particularly, into essentially a purchasing pool of health care so as to be able to give individuals and small businesses the collective purchasing power of big business with its competitive advantage of being able to lower rates and to offer more choice at the same time in a competitive situation I think is an outstanding idea.

I have always favored it, and I think that the more the Government can do to promote the expansion of regional alliances for people to join voluntarily, then the more, bit by bit, we will reduce the number of people who are not insured in this country.

One more thing, Mr. Chairman. I have to say to the witnesses with some apologies, you can see that there are not too many members here today. In fact, I will have to be leaving in a little bit. The House of Representatives changed its schedule last night and that has affected everything we are doing today.

But I want to stress to you as witnesses that the effect of your testimony is not whether there are one, two, three, or four members of a subcommittee listening to you face to face, but the fact that everything you say and everything you enter in writing goes into the record and is made available to all of our colleagues throughout the House of Representatives and throughout the Senate as they make judgments on this situation. So I ask you to keep in mind that your testimony remains to the entire Congress.

With that, I yield back, Mr. Chairman.

Mr. TOWNS. Thank you very much, Mr. Schiff.

Mr. TOWNS. At this time I would like to call our first witness, Mr. Mark Nadel, associate director of health financing and policy issues at the General Accounting Office.

Mr. Nadel, it is the custom of this committee to swear in its witnesses. Also, I would like to—being participants, I would like to swear them in as well. Their names, could you give us their names?

Mr. FAIRBANKS. Tim Fairbanks.

Mr. OCHINKO. Walter Ochinko.

Mr. TOWNS. Do you swear that the testimony you will give is the truth, the whole truth, and nothing but the truth? If so, answer in the affirmative.

[A chorus of "I do."]

[Witnesses sworn].

Mr. TOWNS. I would like to welcome you to the subcommittee. And without objection, your entire statement will be included in the record. If you could summarize within 5 minutes, which will allow the committee the opportunity to raise some questions with you. You may proceed.

STATEMENT OF MARK NADEL, ASSOCIATE DIRECTOR, HEALTH FINANCING AND POLICY ISSUES, GENERAL ACCOUNTING OFFICE, ACCOMPANIED BY TIM FAIRBANKS AND WALTER OCHINKO

Mr. NADEL. Thank you, Mr. Chairman.

I am pleased to be here to testify on our report on "Health Purchasing Cooperatives" which we undertook at your request.

I am accompanied this morning by Tim Fairbanks and Walter Ochinko, who worked very hard on this study.

One of the few facts agreed upon by all sides in today's health reform debate is that small businesses have a tough time buying and keeping health insurance for their employees. Some small groups cannot obtain insurance at any price, while others can pay up to 40 percent more to get the same coverage as larger firms.

One response to this problem has been to pool the buying power of individual small firms. Just as hardware store owners, farmers and other small business owners have formed co-ops to use their combined power to buy merchandise at a lower price, so too are we seeing the rise of insurance purchasing cooperatives around the country.

And the basic principle is that large numbers of small firms can join together to reduce their administrative expenses, pool their insurance risk and increase their clout in the market to get a better deal. These co-ops can be public, which are composed of State or local agencies, private, composed of small or large businesses, or State chartered systems that combine public and private employers and potentially Medicaid recipients.

Regardless of the outcome of the current national health reform debate, the growing number of States and businesses forming cooperatives suggest that they are here to stay. We have found, as you pointed out, that pool purchasing is both a tested and effective mechanism to address recognized problems in the insurance market, particularly for small employers.

Purchasing co-ops have several administrative functions in common, including enrollment, premium collection and contracting with health plans, and these functions are similar to those being considered for voluntary co-ops by the Congress. But existing cooperatives throughout the country are also empowered to provide additional policy and management functions, and it is on these that I would like to focus this morning.

First, existing co-ops often play an active role in designing the benefit package. For example, the State legislature gave the Health Insurance Plan of California, properly known as Hipick or HIPC, it gave them responsibility for developing the benefits package offered to small employers and HIPC created a standardized benefit structure.

Now, a standardized benefit package is useful because it enables consumers to compare plans, and it also helps prevent plans from gaming the benefit structure to avoid higher health risks or otherwise unfairly discriminate.

Second, co-ops have significant power over the type and number of participating health insurance carriers and thus over consumer choice.

The publicly charted cooperatives offer more plans than the private cooperatives we visited. For example, HIPC offers enrollees a choice of 18 competing insurance carriers. On the other hand, the Council of Smaller Employers in Cleveland, known as COSE, which is typical of the private cooperatives we visited, contracts with only two carriers.

The third function is a particularly controversial issue in the consideration of cooperatives: Whether they should negotiate premiums with insurance carriers.

Now, some versions of the managed competition concept view co-ops as more neutral with competition between health plans itself serving to hold down prices. Most existing cooperatives, however, view their ability to negotiate directly with carriers as a critical tool for holding down health insurance premium growth. Despite their belief that competition among plans is key to achieving reasonable premium growth, public co-ops have recently begun to augment market forces with price negotiations.

For example, in Wisconsin and California, after the co-ops were fairly passive recipients of significant premium increases through the 1980's, they recently turned to a tough negotiating strategy, and afterwards premium increases were substantially less than they had been previously.

The private co-ops we visited also believe that their negotiating hand is greatly strengthened by severely restricting the number of participating carriers. Although they may solicit bids from a number of competitors they approach negotiations with the implicit caveat that they will award the contract to only a limited number or a single competitor. For example, COSE in Cleveland contracts with only two carriers to obtain a volume discount, and consequently, COSE accounts for 15 percent of the business of Blue Cross/Blue Shield in its market area, which obviously gives it considerable leverage.

A final and important function of co-ops are programs to measure, improve and report on the quality of care delivered by participating plans. But these programs, however, are only in their infancy. When mandatory alliances were proposed there was concern about there being big bureaucracies. However, we found that they are not big bureaucracies. Their operating costs range, at the upper end, from about 3 percent of premium down to less than 1 percent.

To many Americans, purchasing co-ops are an unfamiliar new entity which raise legitimate concerns about the role of government, employers and employees in their operation. Governance is a central issue because cooperatives could be the vehicle through which many Americans would obtain portable health benefits.

Therefore it is important to ensure public and private accountability.

A good example of some of these problems was Florida, which sought to achieve accountability through balanced representation on the boards but through politicization has had some trouble achieving that end. Politicization with the potential to undermine public confidence in cooperatives suggest that Congress should pay serious attention to provisions regarding governance.

In conclusion, Mr. Chairman, regardless of the outcome of the debate over cooperatives and national reform proposals, pool purchasing appears to be an increasingly accepted mechanism to address insurance market shortcomings. If cooperatives are to become a national vehicle for expanding insurance coverage, however, Congress may want to give greater attention to the selection, composition and accountability of cooperative governing boards.

Mr. Chairman, that concludes my statement. I would be happy to answer any questions.

Mr. TOWNS. Thank you very much for your testimony.

[The prepared statement of Mr. Nadel follows:]

Mr. Chairman and Members of the Subcommittee:

I am pleased to be here to testify on our report on health insurance purchasing cooperatives, a study that we undertook at your request.[1]

One of the few facts agreed upon by all sides in today's health reform debate is that small businesses and other small organizations have had a tough time buying and keeping health insurance for their employees. Some small groups cannot obtain insurance at any price because of the health status of just one of their employees. Even those able to secure coverage may face very high premiums because their health costs are unpredictable and the costs attributable to one sick person must be borne entirely by each small group. Because risk can't be spread and because of relatively higher overhead, it can cost up to 40 percent more for a small firm to get the same coverage as a larger firm.

One response to this problem is to pool the buying power of individual small firms. Just as hardware store owners, farmers, and other small business owners have formed cooperatives and other associations to use joint purchasing power to buy merchandise at a lower price than they could do individually, so too have we seen the rise of insurance purchasing cooperatives around the country. The basic principle of such cooperatives is that large numbers of

---

[1]<u>Access to Health Insurance: Public and Private Employers' Experience with Purchasing Cooperatives</u> (GAO/HEHS-94-142, May 31, 1994).

relatively small organizations can join together to reduce their administrative expenses, pool their insurance risk, and increase their clout in the market to get a better deal.

The original Clinton administration proposal called for mandatory cooperatives, called alliances, but sentiment in the Congress is now clearly toward voluntary cooperatives. While the Congress has been deliberating health care reform, including the role of cooperatives, state governments and private organizations throughout the nation have been forming and operating such cooperatives. Increasingly, voluntary purchasing cooperatives will be the vehicle by which small business provides health insurance. Therefore, you asked us to examine the operation, authority, and accountability of existing cooperatives. Our objective was to inform the Congress on issues that might arise as it moves toward enacting legislation that could make such cooperatives a much more important part of the health care environment.

BACKGROUND

Cooperatives can be public, private, or state chartered systems that include public and private employers, and potentially Medicaid recipients.[2]

---

[2]The 11 purchasing cooperatives we visited and some of their characteristics are listed in table 1.

- **Private cooperatives** are voluntary associations of
  employers who band together to purchase insurance for their
  employees. Although pooled purchasing is generally
  discussed in the context of assisting small businesses, in
  fact, large firms have also organized cooperatives.
  Examples of private cooperatives are the Business Health
  Care Action Group, a relatively new association of large
  Minneapolis-based firms, and the Council of Smaller
  Enterprises (COSE), a small employer association founded in
  1973.

- **Public cooperatives** were originally established by state
  governments to purchase insurance for state employees and
  were subsequently expanded to allow voluntary participation
  by county and municipal workers or other public entities.
  The largest public cooperative we visited, the California
  Public Employees' Retirement System (CalPERS), began
  offering health insurance over 30 years ago and now has
  nearly 1 million covered lives.[3] Recently, several states
  have again expanded public programs by creating voluntary
  cooperatives targeted at small businesses.

- Finally, **statewide systems of cooperatives** being
  established in some parts of the country are an amalgam of

---

[3]Health Insurance: California Public Employees' Alliance Has
Reduced Recent Premium Growth (GAO/HRD-94-40, Nov. 22, 1993).

public and private cooperatives. They will eventually
embrace state employees and Medicaid recipients and are
open on a voluntary basis to a wider spectrum of groups,
including private firms, the self-employed, and low-income
individuals. The farthest along is Florida's statewide
system of 11 regional cooperatives that began enrolling
members in May 1994.

Table 1: Membership and Enrollment of Purchasing Cooperatives
          GAO Visited

Public Cooperatives

California Public Employees' Retirement System (CalPERS)	State and local government employees	**930,000**
Washington State Health Care Authority		
Public Employees Benefit Board	State and school district employees	265,824
Basic Health Plan	Individuals on subsidies and those willing to join on a nonsubsidized basis	32,697
Caregivers	Caregivers	50
Total		**298,571**
Health Insurance Plan of California (HIPC)	Firms with 5-50 full-time employees	**44,000**
Minnesota Department of Employee Relations		
State Employee Insurance Program	State employees	144,000-
Public Employee Insurance Program	Local government employees	5,000
Minnesota Employers Insurance Program	Private employers with two or more .employees	1,000
Total		**150,000**
Wisconsin State Employee Group Health Benefits Program	State and local government employees	**195,000**

Private Cooperatives

Business Health Care Action Group (BHCAG), Minnesota	Firms with more than 500 employees	**45,000**
Council of Smaller Enterprises (COSE), Ohio	Firms with fewer than 151 employees	**200,000**
Employers Association Buyers' Coalition, Minnesota	Small- to medium-sized firms	**13,000**
Employers Health Purchasing Cooperative, Washington	Small and large firms	**1,050**

Statewide Cooperative Systems

Florida	Firms with fewer than 51 employees, state workers, and individuals eligible for subsidies	Enrollment began mid-May 1994
Washington	Individuals and any size firm	Not yet enrolling

Regardless of the outcome of the current national health reform debate, the growing number of states and businesses forming cooperatives suggests they are here to stay. We found that pooled purchasing is both a tested and effective mechanism to address recognized problems in the insurance market--especially for small employers.

EXISTING COOPERATIVES HAVE BROAD AUTHORITY OVER HEALTH INSURANCE ADMINISTRATION AND BENEFITS

Purchasing cooperatives have several administrative functions in common including enrollment, premium collection, and contracting with health plans. These functions are similar to those being considered for voluntary cooperatives by the Congress. But existing cooperatives are also empowered to perform additional policy and management functions. Notable among the broad policy functions assigned to existing cooperatives are the ability to (1) define benefits packages, (2) include or exclude individual health plans, (3) negotiate contracts, and (4) develop and analyze quality data.

Benefits Package

Existing cooperatives often play an active role regarding benefits. The state legislature gave the Health Insurance Plan of California (HIPC) responsibility for developing the benefits package offered to small employers. Using health maintenance organization licensing standards and information gathered during a series of public hearings, HIPC created a standardized benefit structure. Other cooperatives have also standardized benefits in order to (1) prevent plans from using the benefit structure to deter bad risk enrollees, (2) make it easier for consumers to compare plans, and finally (3) enable the cooperative staff to more easily eValuate each plan's efficiency. Private cooperatives generally work with insurance carriers to develop benefit structures that reflect the needs of their membership.

Contracting Authority Affects Consumer Choice

CooperatiVes have significant power over the type and number of participating health insurance carriers and thus over consumer choice. Although states allow public cooperatives to exclude carriers, they tend to be inclusive. Thus, HIPC offers enrollees a choice of 18 competing carriers. Especially for small businesses, the broad choice of plans offered by public cooperatives expands the options available to their employees. On the other hand, COSE, typical of the priVate cooperatives we Visited, contracts with only two carriers.

Because they believe managed care is more effective at controlling costs, both the private and public cooperatives we visited generally offer managed care options to enrollees. In 1983, the Wisconsin cooperative announced that, with the exception

of its two self-funded fee-for-service (FFS) plans, only health
maintenance organizations (HMO) would be allowed to participate.
Enrollment in HMOs more than tripled to 65 percent the next year.
Officials at Cleveland-based COSE told us that their members prefer
FFS plans and that this preference has limited the cooperatives'
ability to more actively encourage enrollment in plans with
stronger cost control features. Only 21 percent of COSE members
are enrolled in HMOs.

Negotiating Authority

A particularly controversial issue in the consideration of
cooperatives is whether they should negotiate premiums with
insurance carriers. Some versions of managed competition view
cooperatives as more neutral, with competition between health plans
serving to hold down prices. Most existing cooperatives, however,
view their ability to negotiate with carriers as a critical tool
for restraining growth in health insurance premiums.

Despite their belief that competition among plans is key to
achieving reasonable premium growth, public cooperatives have
recently begun to augment market forces with price negotiations.
The Wisconsin cooperative adopted a number of cost control measures
in 1983 but simply accepted sealed bids from health plans without
any discussion of premium increases. Over the next decade,
initially low yearly premium increases were followed by several

years of significantly accelerated premium growth. Wisconsin
turned to negotiations in 1993. The cooperative hired an actuary
to develop target premiums for each plan based on data submitted by
health carriers. If a plan's bid was significantly higher than its
target, cooperative officials discussed the discrepancy with plan
representatives. Wisconsin officials told us that best-and-final
offers from 9 of the 10 plans contacted for discussion had
substantially lower premiums.

Although CalPERS had long discussed premium increases with
health plans, pressure to contain costs became critical in 1991
when California froze the state contribution to premiums,
magnifying the impact of rate increases on state employees. As a
result, CalPERS began aggressive negotiations with health plans in
1992 and had held premium increases to well below the national
average. Another California cooperative, HIPC, recently achieved a
6-percent reduction over premiums offered in 1993, its first year
of operation.

The private purchasing cooperatives we visited believe that
their negotiating hand is strengthened by severely restricting the
number of participating carriers. Although they may solicit bids
from a number of competitors, private cooperatives approach
negotiations with the implicit caveat that they will award the
contract to a single competitor. For example, COSE, a private
small business cooperative, contracts with only two carriers to

obtain a Volume discount. Constituting about 15 percent of Blue
Cross's business in the Cleveland metropolitan area, COSE is the
carrier's single largest customer. According to COSE officials,
Blue Cross knows that the cooperative could "shop around" when the
current contract expires.

Quality of Care

Reflecting the state of the art, programs to measure, improve,
and report on the quality of care delivered by participating health
plans are in their infancy. Compared to the public cooperatives we
visited, howeVer, private purchasing pools placed more emphasis on
such programs. For example, the Business Health Care Action Group
sponsored creation of a $2 million institute to develop practice
guidelines and a system to monitor treatment and patient outcomes.
Public cooperatiVes are now beginning programs that focus on the
quality of the serVices obtained. Officials at the Minnesota State
cooperatiVe told us that they intend to create a new unit to
collect and analyze quality outcomes data. Florida's statewide
system of cooperatiVes will issue report cards on quality using
health plan data analyzed by a state agency.

EXISTING COOPERATIVES OPERATE
WITH MODEST BUDGETS AND STAFFS

Existing cooperatives are not big bureaucracies. Their
operating costs range from about 3 percent of total insurance

premiums for smaller or recently formed cooperatives such as the
HIPC, to less than 1 percent of premiums for larger and more mature
purchasing pools like the Wisconsin State Employee Group Health
Benefits Program. Most cooperatives contract with private firms
for enrollment and premium collection activities. Their relatively
modest in-house staffs tend to focus on management and policy
functions, including premium negotiations, plan monitoring, and
contractor oversight.

CONCERNS REMAIN REGARDING GOVERNING STRUCTURES

To many Americans, purchasing cooperatives are an unfamiliar
new entity, raising legitimate concerns about the role of
government, employers, and employees in their operation.
Governance is a central issue because under many reform proposals
cooperatives are the vehicle through which many Americans would
obtain portable health benefits. And for those unable to obtain or
afford insurance under the current system, government subsidies
channeled through purchasing cooperatives would facilitate access
to coverage. This nexus of interests highlights the importance of
establishing a proper balance between public and private
accountability. Although many of the cooperatives we visited
provide limited lessons for establishing such accountability, we
believe that the experience of Florida cooperatives identifies some
of the potential pitfalls.

- Although the Florida law requires that cooperative boards reflect the demographics of the population served, that goal has been difficult to achieve. Political rivalry among the three appointing officials has impeded the coordination needed to meet the law's goal.

- The "consumer" representatives on the boards--defined in the law as "an individual user of health care services"-- are virtually indistinguishable from the 11 statutory "business" representatives.

- According to a Florida official, inadequate screening resulted in board members whose appointments could be challenged--for example, appointees with prohibited affiliations such as health care consulting.

Politicization, with the potential to undermine public confidence in purchasing cooperatives, suggests that serious attention should be paid to provisions regarding the composition and appointment of boards. Florida's experience suggests that in providing for cooperatives the Congress should include a mechanism to ensure achievement of any representational goals.

CONCLUSION

Regardless of the outcome of the debate over cooperatives in national reform proposals, pooled purchasing appears to be an increasingly accepted mechanism to address insurance market shortcomings. Our work suggests that the criticism of purchasing cooperatives as too regulatory and too bureaucratic has been overstated. Cooperatives are a proven and economical way for firms, especially small employers, to purchase insurance. If cooperatives become a national vehicle for expanding insurance coverage, however, the Congress may want to give greater attention to the selection, composition, and accountability of cooperative governing boards.

Mr. Chairman, this concludes my statement. I would be happy to answer any questions.

(108210)

Mr. TOWNS. Let me begin by first asking you how does the average person or business become a member of an alliance? And maybe you can add, so how do they select a health plan as well?

Mr. NADEL. Well, there would be several ways. Typically, particularly with the large public alliances such as Florida, which has just formed, they would advertise. They have to do some marketing, just as an insurance company would, and they would go out to businesses and say we are here, we are offering insurance, and the business would contact the alliance and join, or the alliance could contact all the businesses of the size category it is reaching and point out the advantages.

Then having selected insurance plans to contract with, the alliance offers the employer a menu of plans, and the employer would choose the plan. It is also possible, of course, for the employees to individually choose, but right now it is more typical for the employers to choose.

Mr. FAIRBANKS. I would just add to that, that in a number of cases alliances have provided for brokers or agents to work for them and receive commissions. The HIPC in California——

Mr. NADEL. And Florida.

Mr. FAIRBANKS [continuing]. And Florida also provide for brokers to sell the alliance members insurance.

Mr. TOWNS. What evidence do you have that alliances are effective in terms of controlling costs? Do you have any evidence that you could present?

Mr. NADEL. That is actually a more complicated question than many people realize. It is an excellent question because we have found that, for example, in California, what is probably the largest cooperative, CalPERS, did have several years of cost increases which were actually higher than both the national and State avera es. After they started negotiating, those increases went way dgwn.

In 1993, for example, they were 1½ percent, and in 1994 there actually was a decrease in premiums. But that is not a complete answer by itself because premium growth has been held down throughout the country, even in nonalliances. So it is difficult to know what would have happened in the absence of alliances.

Also, as is well-known, California had a major, State financial crisis, and so basically the State simply said, "We are not going to pay any more, period." And since they were insuring 900,000 lives that gave them quite a bit of bargaining clout. In more normal circumstances they may not have had that kind of leverage.

But with those qualifications, and I hate to be sort of, you know, mealymouthed about the answer, but it is just important to know that just because they did significantly decrease premium growth, and the same in Wisconsin, we can't attribute it only to alliances. But we think the evidence does suggest, based particularly on the Wisconsin and the California experience—COSE also has had considerably lower premium growth than private companies which are not in the alliance. So we think there is pretty strong evidence that they held down growth.

Mr. TOWNS. I guess politicians don't generally say this too much, but I think that the alliance is overly political, and I think that we agree to that. I see a great danger in that the political powerless may be totally excluded from these boards—people that have no power.

Who should be represented on the alliance board? And how can we ensure a more balanced system in terms of appointments?

In other words, we would have the handicapped, senior citizens, women—just a whole cross section. How do we get that balance?

Mr. NADEL. We think that the experience of Florida and CalPERS may offer some examples. Florida does require representation in terms of there being some consumer representation. They also try to acquire demographic or ethnic representation by having—making sure there is representation of minorities.

As I have pointed out, though, they have had a little trouble in achieving that because the boards are appointed by three different entities, three different political entities, and so it is hard to achieve that kind of balance when you have three people making the appointments. They may have had trouble doing that.

In California, the board does require elected employee members as well. So that is another possibility.

I do not think that we can recommend a particular way to balance it. I think what we are saying is that as Congress enacts legislation providing for alliances some consideration should be given to making sure that consumers are represented, that there are conflict of interest provisions.

Mr. TOWNS. You know, there is a lot of talk going on as we debate the health care bill here that refer to the alliances as big bureaucracies. But you have indicated the fact is that is not the case in terms of the ones you visited. Could you talk about the staff size of these alliances, the ones that you visited?

Mr. NADEL. Sure. They ranged from, at the bottom, about just 2 people, the small ones, and the largest ones, in California and in Washington State, had only 95 people. Another way to look at it is the number of people compared to the amount of business they do. And at the largest their overhead costs were about—for the mature ones were about 1 percent of premiums.

You are always going to get somewhat larger as they are starting up because there are some fixed costs. But generally they are not that large. And one thing that accounts for differences in size is, obviously, how much they do. Many of the private and smaller alliances contract out routine functions like enrollment, premium collection. They would do that with a third party administrator, typical of what many businesses do now, and that would hold down their size.

But we certainly didn't find them to be large, overwhelming bureaucratic entities. Even the largest one, California, which covers nearly a million lives, you know, has less than 100 employees.

Mr. TOWNS. Thank you very much.

At this time I yield to Congressman Schiff.

Mr. SCHIFF. Thank you, Mr. Chairman.

Mr. Chairman, I have no questions of the panel. I appreciate their testimony, and once again emphasize just for the record that I am not and I know of nobody who is criticizing regional purchasing alliances. I think they are a fine idea.

The issue in Congress is should people be required to join a particular alliance. It is to that I object.

Thank you, Mr. Chairman. I yield back.

Mr. TOWNS. Thank you very much.

Let me thank you, Mr. Nadel, and let me thank all of you for your participation, and we look forward to working with you further as we continue to debate this issue.

Mr. NADEL. Thank you very much, Mr. Chairman, Mr. Schiff.

Mr. TOWNS. Our next panel is Douglas Cook, director of the Florida Agency for Health Care Administration; Steven Wetzell, executive director of the Business Health Care Action Group in Minnesota; Jason Adkins, executive director of the Center for Insurance Research in Massachusetts.

Gentlemen, it is the policy of this committee to swear in its witnesses. So, if you would stand and raise your right hand.

Do you swear the testimony you will give is the truth, the whole truth and nothing but the truth? If so, answer in the affirmative?

[A chorus of "I do"].

[Witnesses sworn].

Mr. TOWNS. Take your seats.

I would like to welcome all of you to the subcommittee. We have your prepared statement which, without objection, will be included in the record. We would like for you to proceed in terms of summarizing your testimony within 5 minutes so that the members will have an opportunity to raise questions with you.

So, Mr. Cook, why don't you begin?

STATEMENTS OF DOUGLAS COOK, DIRECTOR, FLORIDA AGENCY FOR HEALTH CARE ADMINISTRATION; STEVEN WETZELL, EXECUTIVE DIRECTOR, BUSINESS HEALTH CARE ACTION GROUP, MINNESOTA; AND JASON ADKINS, EXECUTIVE DIRECTOR, CENTER FOR INSURANCE RESEARCH, MASSACHUSETTS

Mr. COOK. Thank you very much, Mr. Chairman.

First of all, let me thank you, Mr. Chairman, for the outstanding work that your committee has done on health care. You, as we know, have been in south Florida looking at some of the significant problems we have with fraud and abuse in some Federal programs. You have been extremely helpful and have shown great leadership, and we thank you and your committee staff for the outstanding work you have done.

The Governor asked me to pass on his personal thanks to you for coming to south Florida and bringing attention to those problems.

Mr. TOWNS. Thank you.

Mr. COOK. We faced a unique problem in Florida, Mr. Chairman, as you learned in your visit. Over the period of the 1980's we experienced cost growth in our health insurance programs exceeding 20 percent a year during that time. Thousands of Floridians lost their health insurance as a result of that.

Thousands of businesses were prevented from purchasing health insurance, and Florida is a unique State in that we are a small business State. Unlike many States of the Northeast, most of our businesses, in fact, 95 percent of our businesses, are businesses with less than 25 employees. So, without large businesses you have been able to leverage their purchasing in the free market.

Many of our businesses have gone without health insurance. In fact, 50—only 55 percent of all Florida businesses provide health insurance. That leaves over 40,000 Florida businesses which provide no health insurance to their employees.

We have the fourth highest uninsured rate in the country. Over 22 percent for folks under the age of 65. That uninsurance, of course, increases costs, because the costs from the uninsured are passed on to the insured. And as you know, Mr. Chairman, over 80 percent of the uninsured folks in this country are working folks and their families.

This is not a problem of the very poor, and it certainly is not a problem of the very rich. In fact, a Palm Beach Post editorial recently indicated that some of the plans in Congress and some of the plans that we were seeing were more like suggesting that "people take two aspirins and call when they are rich."

The fact of the matter is working people and their families are the people who are denied health insurance, and without some means of leveraging this market they will never be able to purchase it.

Florida also has the unique and kind of unfortunate problem of having three of the five most expensive Medicare per admission rates in the country, according to the Urban Institute and the New England Journal of Medicine in an article published in March of last year they cited Miami, Fort Lauderdale, and Tampa as the 1, 2, and No. 5 cities in terms of the Medicare per admission rate.

Again, that has a lot to do with the fact that we have a substantial elder population. We have a medical industry which has organized itself to serve that elder population, and in many cases underserve that elder population, and the costs of our uninsured are passed on to the insured, and we are not able to organize our system in any kind of logical way. So, we had a lot of good reasons to take up health care reform.

Last year, our legislature passed our landmark Healthy Homes Act, and Governor Chiles had worked very hard at establishing 11 community health purchasing alliances, which roughly corresponded to the 11 major metropolitan areas of the State. You will see in my testimony, I think at page 2 of the testimony, a map which delineates those alliances, and you can see that Dade County or Miami, Broward County, Fort Lauderdale, Palm Beach, Jacksonville, Orlando, Tampa, St. Petersburg, Fort Myers, and Pensacola—the major metropolitan areas of the State along with two of our rural areas, Gainesville and Tallahassee, make up our regional purchasing alliances.

We chose, and I understand the concerns that you have expressed, Mr. Chairman, and greatly respect those concerns. We chose to move initially with politically appointed boards, and there was a purpose for that. That was not a compromise that we had to make in the process. That was something that we well considered beforehand. And that was in getting these alliances off the ground we wanted to insure that there was some political accountability.

I know that political has become a negative word in our public lexicon these days. However, I worked for a man who has been a politician for 30 years and he kind of likes being called a politician.

He happens to think that the people put him there and he ought to be held accountable for his actions.

I think that the testimony, the previous testimony you heard expressing some concerns that there are three appointers to the boards implied that one of the appointers—in fact, the Governor—was very representative in his appointments.

All of his board appointments, and they make up 9 of the 17 board appointments, are broadly representative of the age, racial and gender specifics of each of our districts. However, as the GAO pointed out, some of the other—the other two appointers might not have been as aggressive in looking at that. So, that is certainly a concern.

But I guess the Governor's concern and his reason for moving initially with political appointments was that he wanted somebody held accountable. He wanted somebody held accountable for the quality of the appointment, for the diversity of the appointment, and for, ultimately, the outcome of what the board produced in terms of health reform.

He wanted people to know that his nine appointments were representative of the kinds of people that he wanted to serve on this board, and he wanted to be held accountable for the results that they produced.

He also, because he was forced to make one compromise—he was going to be the sole appointing authority initially, and one of the compromises was to allow the Speaker of the House and our President of the Senate, in due respect to the legislative process, to appoint four members apiece. He wants them held accountable for their appointments, the diversity of their appointments and the outcomes of their appointments.

So, to just address that, we happen to think that that is not necessarily a negative thing, and we do believe that Congress ought to look at the outcomes produced from these boards. If they produce lower prices, if they produce higher health care, and if they don't allow their political affiliation to interfere with their duties, then they have done the job.

On the other hand, if they don't do the job that they need to do, then the Congress can look at them very seriously and that is why you have the GAO and other outstanding arms to look into how a State or region applies that.

Let me kind of briefly summarize because I know you have got distinguished panel members and I know in your questions——

Mr. TOWNS. And the red light is on.

Mr. COOK. Sir.

Mr. TOWNS. And the red light is on.

Mr. COOK. OK. Then I will do it in 30 seconds, Mr. Chairman.

Without alliances small businesses will not have the choice nor the leverage in the market. There is absolutely no way that a small business with 3 employees or 5 employees or 10 employees can afford the benefits manager, can afford the shopping, can afford to bring the pressure to bear that you need to bring to bear to do it.

If you look at Florida's alliances, and I hope some of our questions bring it out, if you look at the—excuse me—page 8 of my testimony, what you will see is a Statewide summary of what the alliances, the outcomes the alliances initially produced. For 11 alliances, the average number of carriers was over 28 carriers or AHPs—accountable health plans. There were over 120 choices offered to alliance members. Now, any small business in America will tell you today that they are lucky to have 2 or 3 choices much less 120 choices.

If you look at the number of plans that reduced prices, and we based this on what an average price was in that geographical area, over 70 percent of the plans offered in the average CHPA area reduced prices from what the folks were currently paying that day.

And, in fact, maybe the most outstanding example we have of that—and reduced prices, by the way, somewhere in the order of 25 to 40 percent. So, the fact that the prices are posted, the fact that the prices are compared, and the fact that the CHPAs and purchasing alliances offer the buying/purchasing is something very significant.

One of the great problems you have in the health insurance market today is that people don't know, and without that knowledge— without that knowledge of choice, without that ability to comparison shop, you can't reduce prices. Choice is a major thing. Reduction of prices is a major thing.

Mr. TOWNS. Your 30 seconds are also up.

Mr. COOK. Yes, sir.

[The prepared statement of Mr. Cook follows:]

Douglas M. Cook, Director
Florida Agency for Health Care Administration

Testimony Before the Human Resources
and Intergovernmental Relations Subcommittee
of the Committee on Government Operations

The Honorable Edolphus Towns, Chairman

June 30, 1994

Chairman Towns and members of the subcommittee, thank you for the opportunity to come to Washington and report on our early successes with health insurance purchasing alliances in Florida.

As you know, Florida initiated its current health care reform activities under the leader-ship of Governor Lawton Chiles with the passage of the Health Care Reform Act of 1992. This legislation set the stage for a voluntary public/private partnership that has begun to expand access to basic health benefits and gain control of our runaway costs.

Our system of community health purchasing alliances, known as CHPAs (*chippas*) was authorized by our Health Care and Insurance Reform Act of 1993 (Chapter 93-129, Laws of Florida). This legislation established Florida as the first state to test the managed competition reform strategy on a statewide basis.

After enacting the law in April of 1993, we began a careful and detailed process select-ing 11 separate 17-member boards of directors. There were a number of required cri-teria in the board selection process, including residency in the CHPA district, lack of any current or prior affiliation with a health care insurer or provider, adequate repre-sentation from small businesses with 50 or fewer employees, appropriate reflection of the district's demographic diversity, and willingness to serve voluntarily without com-pensation. Appointments were made by the Governor, the President of the Senate, and the Speaker of the House of Representatives by October 1, 1993.

We had a two-day educational retreat for the new board members in November 1993, and by February of this year, the 11 CHPAs had hired staff (one or two people each) and established local offices. The CHPAs released their initial round of requests for proposals to accountable health partnerships (AHPs) in December, and opened bids on February 10th. We received bids submitted by 46 AHPs offering a total of over 1,000 plans. We are very pleased with the diversity of the coverage available to CHPA members, as well as the competitive prices. The average small business can choose from 28 AHPs offering 120 different plans at an average savings of 25 percent.

The CHPAs began enrolling members over the past month, and the system is now fully operational with small businesses purchasing coverage based on the AHP bids. Even without a significant marketing effort, which is slated to begin late this summer, the CHPAs are actively signing up small businesses who recognize a good deal when they see one. A detailed CHPA implementation schedule appears on page 12.

Provisions of the Health Care and Insurance Reform Act of 1993 Regarding Community Health Purchasing Alliances

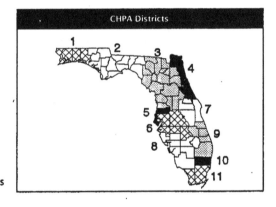

- Florida's 11 community health purchasing alliances (CHPAs) are regional, non-profit organizations with exclusive territories.

- The 17-member voluntary board of directors includes nine gubernatorial appointees and four each by the President of the Senate and the Speaker of the House of Representatives.

- Board members cannot have any affiliation with health care providers or insurers.

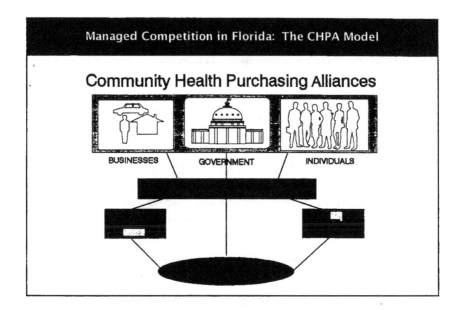

- The CHPAs develop requests for proposals to annually solicit bids from competing insurer/provider networks, called accountable health partnerships, or AHPs.

- Any employer with 1-50 full-time employees is eligible to join the CHPA in its district. Small businesses and others are required to meet the terms of CHPA membership, pay a membership fee, and purchase their health care through the CHPA.

- A CHPA may require a small employer seeking membership to agree to participate in the alliance for a minimum period of time, not to exceed one year.

- Employers must pay a portion of an employee's health insurance premium as a condition of participation in the CHPA. Generally, an employer is required to contribute 50 percent of the premium of the lowest cost plan selected by the employer. Although CHPAs requested bids on zero and 25 percent contribution levels, few if any of these bids were received.

- CHPAs use the annual bids submitted in response to their request for proposals and their price comparison sheets to ensure that AHPs offer competitive prices for their services.

- Employers with 30 or more employees must offer at least three plans to their employees; smaller employers must offer at least two plans.

- CHPAs are responsible for:

  - recruiting members;

  - providing price and quality information on AHPs to their members;

  - offering AHPs to members;

  - handling member grievances against AHPs;

  - providing data to the state (Agency for Health Care Administration) on CHPA operations; and

  - marketing CHPA services.

- CHPAs are authorized to perform the following purchasing services:

  - requesting proposals from all AHPs for standard, basic, and specialized health plans;

  - annually offering to their members only health plans offered by AHPs that submit a responsive proposal, including the information necessary for the completion of AHP comparison sheets;

  - providing assistance to alliance members in selecting and obtaining coverage through AHPs;

  - collecting patient outcome data from AHPs;

  - providing to alliance members clear, standardized information on each AHP and each health plan offered by an AHP; and

- distributing to health care purchasers price data on health care services, including retail prices on prescription drugs, durable medical equipment, and medical supplies.

- CHPAs may not directly negotiate rates with AHPs.

- CHPAs may reject an AHP's offer only if the bid is unresponsive to the CHPA's specifications for comparison of AHP offers. All bids that are responsive to the CHPA's requests for proposals must be offered to alliance members.

- CHPAs distribute AHP comparison sheets to their members so they will have the information they need about services, price, and quality when they and their employees choose AHPs.

- Only alliance members are eligible to purchase health care coverage through the CHPAs. Alliance members may be small businesses with 1-50 full-time employees; state employees; Medicaid recipients; and, when implemented, Florida Health Security participants.

- Coverage is purchased through licensed insurance agents.

- Associate members are employers with more than 50 full-time employees. Associate alliance members can participate on the CHPA board of directors and receive the AHP comparison sheets and other information from the CHPAs.

- Since the CHPA does not assume insurance risk, the AHPs are responsible for member claims.

- To be eligible for health coverage through a CHPA, a self-employed person or independent contractor has to derive taxable income from carrying on a trade or profession and has to have evidence by an IRS 1040 form, Schedule C or F, which shows taxable income in at least one of the two previous years.

- Business health care coalitions cannot join a CHPA, but their members may.

- Before state government employee groups can join a CHPA, the state must consult with collective bargaining organizations, the Department of Management Services, and the administrator of the State Group Insurance Program. The state must ensure that the alliance can offer health plans that meet or exceed the benefit standard that has been collectively bargained. Legislative approval of CHPA membership for the State Employees' Health Insurance Program is required unless:

- employee benefits remain the same or are improved,

- the quality of care is increased, and

-. there is no additional cost to the state or its employees.

♦ Before Medicaid recipient groups can join a CHPA, the state must consult with the Legislature, ensure that CHPA membership will not reduce Medicaid recipient benefits or increase their costs, and obtain federal approval.

♦ CHPAs in areas that are primarily rural can merge, increasing the pool of potential members.

♦ Three or fewer CHPAs located in contiguous districts that are not primarily urban can merge into a single alliance with state approval. Approval depends on a determination that alliance members will be better served by creating a combined alliance.

♦ Short of merger, alliances can form networks with other alliances to improve member services. This may include sharing information systems and the development and costs of other alliance services.

♦ If a CHPA is found to be out of compliance with state law, the state can reconstitute the CHPA, certify a new CHPA, or ask another CHPA to assume responsibility for its territory.

Strengths and Weaknesses of the Law

Overall, we are very pleased with the way our system is progressing. In setting up the alliances, we wanted to achieve three basic goals:

- expanded choice of coverage for CHPA members;
- better prices than CHPA members have been paying previously; and
- better prices than those that are available outside of the CHPAs.

As the data on the following pages shows, we have met each of these goals. The strengths of our approach include:

- Expanded coverage choices at favorable rates for CHPA members. The statewide summary tables on the following pages profile the choices and prices that are available to the average small business in our alliance system. The first table (page 8) provides average figures for a hypothetical small business, illustrating that the typical CHPA member could expect to choose from 28 competing plans. In fact, a total of 46 carriers out of 60 to 70 carriers in the state's small employer market submitted bids in one or more CHPA district.

  Approximately 36 percent of the small group standard bids have premiums that fall below the statewide benchmark. Health plans priced lower than the statewide benchmark occur in every district. The highest number of plans (70) with premiums below the benchmark are available in District 6, which includes the city of Tampa and adjacent rural counties.

  The second table (page 9) illustrates the wide choice of diverse, favorably priced coverage that is available to CHPA members across the state.

Other strengths of our program are:

- Voluntary board members who serve without compensation bring much needed energy and dedication to our overall health care reform efforts.

- The relatively small size of our alliance districts ensures a productive focus on local health issues. We have largely avoided any geographic controversies.

- Our system encourages diverse local participation. A provision of our law, for example, requires the expansion of minority providers in AHPs, which would be very difficult to accomplish without a local presence.

- Start-up funds of $275,000 for each CHPA that were appropriated by the legislature have been crucial to their early operation.

STATEWIDE SUMMARY
Average of All Sample Companies
(Average Size = 16 Employees, Average Premium = $4,329.10)

Number of AHPs Available	28
Number of Plans Offered	120
Number of Plans by Benefit Level	
Basic	34
Standard	86
Number of Plans by Type	
Preferred Provider Organization (PPO)	52
Point of Service (POS)	4
Indemnity	42
Exclusive Provider Organization (EPO)	1
Health Maintenance Organization (HMO)	21

Plans With Lower Premiums

Number of Plans by Benefit Level:	
Small Employer Group - Basic	28
Small Employer Group - Standard	51
Number of Standard Plans by Type:	
PPO	26
HMO	7
Indemnity	16
Other Plans (EPO, POS)	2

Monthly and Percentage Savings

Average Savings for All Plans	$1,098.50	25%
Lowest Cost Standard Plan - HMO	$2,706.74	37%
Lowest Cost Standard Plan - PPO	$1,972.66	54%
Average Savings from Lower Cost Standard HMOs	$1,111.16	26%
Average Savings from Lower Cost Standard PPOs	$1,188.09	27%
Average Per Member Per Month Savings Standard HMO	$ 73.56	27%
Average Per Member Per Month Savings Standard PPO	$68.12	25%

		Plans Offered by Type				
CHPA		EPO	HMO	Indemnity	POS	PPO
-1	Pensacola		2	10	2	13
2	Tallahassee		1	5	3	8
3	Gainesville			4	4	16
4	Jacksonville		1		2	5
5	St. Petersburg		5	1	4	18
6	Tampa		13	13	7	37
7	Orlando		8	1	5	21
8	Sarasota		5	14	6	20
9	West Palm Bch.	1	5		1	5
10	Ft. Lauderdale	1	3			
11	Miami	1	12		1	3
TOTAL		3	55	48	35	146
% of Total Plans by Type		1%	19.2%	16.7%	12.2%	50.9%

**Unduplicated Number of Standard Plans
(With Less Than $500 Deductible)
Offered to Sample Companies at a Cost
the Same or Less than the Statewide Benchmark Premium**

- Employers and insurance agents feel more comfortable discussing market issues — such as the "games" carriers are playing — in the local CHPA environment, rather than with a state agency.

- Alliances have been formed with a minimal bureaucracy. Administrative fees of four to six dollars a month per insurance unit compare very favorably with the administrative costs in the general small-group market.

Some of the weaknesses are:

- The exclusion of potential members such as local government, unemployed individuals, and large businesses reduces the number of people who can benefit from purchasing alliances.

- The lack of a negotiating role for the alliances when dealing with competing AHPs on behalf of their members prevents them from getting even better coverage deals.

- Since our alliances are not exclusive, and small employers can purchase coverage in the standard market, we have experienced some "gaming" of the system by carriers. This includes:

  - encouraging agents to place bad risks in CHPAs, even though carriers are required to offer guarantee issue plans inside and outside the alliances;

  - paying lower commissions to agents for business written inside the CHPA, even though the carrier did not reduce premiums to reflect administrative savings; and

  - using "bait and switch" techniques by contacting a potential CHPA member and convincing the employer to purchase more expensive coverage even though benefits may not be significantly greater.

- Public education and outreach is a critical problem that extends beyond marketing. Many of the people who need insurance seem to have little idea of their health coverage rights and responsibilities. More public education and outreach is essential.

Difficulties Implementing CHPAs

- There is a great deal of administrative complexity appointing board members with detailed selection criteria.

- Private organizations with voluntary boards can become surprisingly independent in their outlook and activities.

- Many potential small-business members are very difficult to reach through traditional marketing channels.

Recommendations for Other States

- Ensure start-up funding to give alliances a running start

- Carefully consider the need to balance diverse local concerns and administrative complexity at the state level when determining how many alliance districts to create

- Private insurance reforms such as guarantee issue, community rating, limited pre-existing condition exclusions, and guaranteed renewability play a crucial role in the success of an alliance system.

- Include public education and outreach activities to ensure that important segments of the uninsured population are not overlooked.

Florida CHPA Implementation Schedule	
ACTIVITY	DATE
Health Care and Insurance Reform Act signed by Governor	April 29, 1993
First AHP and CHPA Workshop	July 12, 1993
Managed Competition Advisory Group formed	August 5, 1993
Second AHP and CHPA Workshop	August 24, 1993
Small Employer Focus Groups	September 20, 1993
CHPA boards incorporated	October 6, 1993
Publication of CHPA rule	October 15, 1993
Publication of AHP rule	October 22, 1993
CHPA Academy for board members	October 24-25, 1993
Department of Insurance approves basic/standard plans	November 5, 1993
Workshop held for all potential AHP applicants	November 6, 1993
First AHP application received	December 1, 1993
Small group Request for Proposal (RFP) issued by CHPA	December 17, 1993
RFP for Third Party Administrator (TPA) services issued by CHPA	December 23, 1993
AHP proposers conference (Orlando)	January 6, 1994
CHPA Board Marketing Conference (Orlando)	January 7, 1994
Deadline for TPAs to submit letter of intent to perform services to CHPAs	January 7, 1994
Deadline for receipt of written inquiries from AHPs	January 14, 1994
Deadline for receipt of proposals for Third Party Administrator Services	January 17, 1994
Opening of proposals from TPAs	January 17, 1994
Preliminary evaluation of TPA proposals by CHPA evaluation terms	January 21, 1994
Deadline for receipt of AHP letter of Intent to submit proposal	January 25, 1994
Deadline for CHPA responses to written inquiries from AHPs	January 26, 1994
First AHP approved	January 28, 1994
Executive Directors hired	January-February 1994
Selection of TPA by CHPA boards	February-May 1994
Deadline for receipt of proposals from AHPs	February 10, 1994
Public opening of AHP proposals	February 10, 1994
Publication of comparison sheets	March 28, 1994
Earliest effective date of coverage	May 1, 1994
Last AHP approved	May 2, 1994
AHP rule adopted (59D-2)	May 10, 1994
CHPA rule adopted (59D-1)	May 19, 1994

12

Florida Community Health Purchasing Alliances

News Coverage May-June 1994

Lawton Chiles, Governor
Douglas M. Cook, Director
Agency for Health Care Administration

ORLANDO SENTINEL

A healthy reform for Florida

Health-care reform no longer is a theory in Florida.

It has been reality since last week, when community health purchasing alliances began operations throughout the state. That's reason to rejoice, particularly for the thousands of working people who don't get insurance coverage as a job benefit, because their employers can't afford it.

Indeed, the alliance that serves Orange, Seminole, Osceola and Brevard counties has received requests from more than 1,000 small businesses that want information about how to sign up for coverage.

The beauty of the purchasing-alliance strategy, initiated by Gov. Lawton Chiles, is that it is voluntary and relies on a free-market approach to make health insurance more affordable for small businesses and their employees.

In short, the alliances, which are governed by local businesses, marshal the buying power of a large number of small businesses and others seeking coverage to approach insurance companies and persuade them to create a variety of less-expensive health-coverage plans.

The result is that in Central Florida there are 34 insurance companies that have been certified to provide coverage through the purchasing alliance. More companies are being evaluated for participation in the near future.

What's particularly exciting is that through the purchasing alliance there are 147 health plans that include fee structures whose features range from a $1,000 deductible to a charge of $10 per doctor visit.

So much for those who tried to block the purchasing-alliance approach by predicting that people would not have a choice of health-plan types.

Clearly, that is not the case.

It's also noteworthy that during the past few months there has been a noticeable drop in the cost of many health-insurance coverage plans in Florida.

There's still much more to do to ensure that affordable health care is available to the 2.5 million Floridians who aren't now insured. Getting the health purchasing alliances into operation is an excellent, practical step in that direction.

42

The big experiment starts

The Dade-Monroe Community Health Purchasing Alliance opens for business today. This private. agency, one of 11 statewide, is the core around which revolves Gov. Lawton Chiles's push to provide low and middle income families affordable access to health care.

The Dade-Monroe CHPA is the state's largest — as is its task. If it is to realize its projected 15 percent savings in health care costs, it'll need the continued support both of businesses and the state, which last year chartered the CHPAs. Unfortunately, some lawmakers this year tried to undermine the CHPAs' potential even before they were all up, running, and tallying results.

District 11's serves a diverse region with 65,000 small businesses — half of which provide no health insurance for their employees There are 34 insurers

TO BETTER HEALTH
Dade-Monroe CHPA can work only if employers, lawmakers wish it.

offering employers more than 150 plans.

The CHPA must position itself as the best and least expensive alternative to small businesses that can afford to employ people but not to insure them. When an employer and its workers don't or can't pay for even a portion of their health care needs, the taxpayers do. CHPAs' success must be measured in the savings realized, while getting quality care to the working poor and others. Anything less and they'll be easy prey for those who don't believe they can work.

Though the CHPAs are nonprofit agencies that must generate revenue, the state will provide some funding annually. Therefore, legislators must ensure that each CHPA is doing its job. This year, alas, they used CHPAs more as a pawn for political shenanigans than as a tool to deliver health care.

New health care alliances ready to do business

JACKIE HALLIFAX
Associated Press

TALLAHASSEE — Kerry
Kennedy doesn't have any exper-
in health care reform.

He s just another small busi-
s owner who wants to provide
ical benefits to his workers
who has looked all over for
erage that wouldn't bankrupt
1

Kennedy got a sneak peek last
k into Florida's brave new
Id of managed competition.
ch opens for business Mon-

Oh, man. I am very
pressed." he said. "I had no
going into this meeting what
ould entail."

ne executive director of one
Florida's new regional health
alliances met with Kennedy
his insurance agent to review
plans that would be available
mall employers who join the
ances.

ennedy, who owns a Titus-
: furniture store, found him-
in the national spotlight last
when his health care woes
described by President
ton in his State of the Union
ess to Congress.

ennedy had been hesitant
ut getting his hopes up that
ida's new health alliances
Id make much difference in
medical insurance market
m not a health person I'm
an insurance agent." Ken-
said. "I'm a furniture
"

it after the meeting, he mar-
d at how many choices of
dable plans were available
ugh the alliances. "This is
nitely a change." he said
rning Monday. Kennedy
other small-business employ-
ill be able to enroll in one of
health care alliances across
oa.

e idea is that, by joining
her, the small businesses can
the benefits of volume pur-

chasing enjoyed by big businesses. That's one of the central
concepts of the health care
reform model known as managed
competition.

The Community Health Pur-
chasing Alliances were created by
state lawmakers a year ago.

They're nonprofit, private entities. Although they are state chartered, they are run by 17-member
boards appointed last fall by
Gov. Lawton Chiles and legislative leaders.

Membership is voluntary and
open to self-employed people
and businesses with up to 50
workers.

The alliances can't purchase or
negotiate on behalf of their members. They have to offer all plans
submitted by insurance companies and health maintenance
organizations.

But the alliances can provide
their members with the information to compare plans. Much of
their work will be handled by
outside benefits management
companies hired this spring. -

"You can walk through the
door [Monday], get the comparative rates and begin shopping,"
said Doug Cook, director of the
Agency for Health Care Administration.

Two-thirds of the plans submitted to the alliances had
cheaper premiums than plans
available in the open market,
said Cook. The average drop in
price was 25 percent.

"That seems to me to be a good
deal," he said

As well as lower costs, the plans
offer patient choice, Cook said.
Only 20 percent were closed networks like HMOs. The rest were
either traditional fee-for-service
indemnity plans or preferred
provider organizations, which
have open networks that patients
can leave if they pay a higher
price

Some 50 insurers offered more
than 1,300 health plans, with an
average of 100 plans in each of
the 11 alliance districts.

The coverage purchased by
alliance members will take effect
in June.

Across the state, the directors
and board members of the alliances aren't sure what they're
going to be faced with when they
open for business. Many hope for
a low-key, quiet beginning to give
them time to work out any kinks
before they publicize a grand
opening in the middle of the
month.

"We're designing the road as
we're building it, and we want to
make sure the first day we open it
we don't have bumper-to-
bumper traffic." said Terry
McCorvie, who met with Kennedy last week.

McCorvie is executive director
of the alliance that includes
Orange, Osceola, Seminole and
Brevard counties.

Mary Jane Gallagher chairs the
board that runs the alliance for
Okeechobee, Indian River, St.
Lucie, Martin and Palm Beach
counties.

Some 250 calls from interested
businesses have come in during
the last two months, she said.

"Like any good business, the
first two weeks will be our trial
and error." Gallagher said. "We
want to be ready for the deluge
that we hope to create around
midmonth. Slow but sure."

Small businesses swamp state office for info on new health-care program

By STEVE HART
Senior Staff Writer

Owners of small businesses flooded the Southwest Florida CHPA office with telephone calls Monday seeking information on how to join the state's ground-breaking health-care reform program

But, information was limited

The Community Health Purchasing Alliance (CHPA, pronounced "chippa") office in Punta Gorda was not ready to pass out information on health insurance providers Callers were asked to leave the'r names so information could be mailed to them later this month.

The Florida Department of Health Care Administration, the agency overseeing the new approach to health care in Florida, sent out a reminder Saturday that Monday was the time that small businesses could start enrolling in the program.

The signal may have come a bit early, said District 8 CHPA Executive Vice President Allen Penn who was busy Monday ·fielding telephone calls. Information on rates and coverage won't be available until about May 15, Penn said.

The Punta Gorda office covers District 8, which includes Collier and Lee counties as well as Charlotte, Hendry, Glades, DeSoto and Sarasota counties.

People who call for information will be sent enrollment packages as soon as they are available Penn said the goal remains to have health care plans available for purchase by June 1.

"Today is our official day of opening," Penn said Monday, "But what we don't have yet are the final, absolute, bottom-line rates."

In the meantime, Penn said, small businesses (those with fewer than 50 employees) can call the regional CHPA office and have their names placed on the list to enroll Telephone numbers to call are 1-800-438-2472, 813-639-6664 or 813-639-0116.

Once on the list, the companies will receive an enrollment packet that will include the necessary enrollment forms and any other information available on the day the packets are mailed.

Enrollment in the CHPA will cost the small businesses $25 a year.

Penn said between 300 and 400 companies from Collier County have already asked to be enrolled.

Penn said Monday that a total of 25 companies are offering 153 health-care plans for businesses in Southwest Florida. Each of those plans will have approximately 150 different rates, all based on size of the companies, the demographics and health records of its employees and other factors.

When the initial bids were opened in February, the monthly health-care costs ranged from $644 per month to $1,791 per month for a company of eight employees and from $2,126 per month to $ $6,414 per month for a company of 25 employees.

Until the complete package of rates is approved by the state, the District 8 CHPA won't be able to tell its prospective members exactly how much their health care package will cost them.

The CHPA is the cornerstone of Florida's health care reform. The idea is to use the government-created entity as a broker for small companies who pool their resources to force cheaper health-care rates. Small companies were targeted because over 95 percent of all Floridians are employed by small businesses.

The small companies will join the CHPA and take advantage of the information it provides — choice of plans and track record of the health-care providers. The companies can then, for the first time ever, have a chance to make apples-to-apples kinds of comparisons of the various plans.

By pooling their resources — sheer numbers of employees — the plan will force health-care providers to lower their prices, to compete for the large block of potential customers.

Naples Daily News 5-3-94

Health-care reforms start to yield results

☐ Insurance agents face an uncertain future as the health-care alliances begin to affect consumers.

By Mike Oliver
OF THE SENTINEL STAFF

When the Florida governor dropped in to visit Kerry Kennedy, the Titusville furniture store owner had his insurance agent by his side.

Gov. Lawton Chiles stopped by the Main Street store Tuesday for a press conference among the sofas and mahogany tables. For Chiles it was a public relations coup for his health-care plan as Kennedy, the man singled out in President Clinton's health-care speech last fall, became the first employer issued insurance coverage under Florida's "managed competition" reform plan.

Kennedy's insurance agent, J. Wayne Edens, praised the plan.

Repeat for those who think the above was a misprint: *Insurance agent J. Wayne Edens praised the plan.*

It's true that many of the state's 66,000 health insurance agents, fearing reform would sweep them out of the picture, were among the fiercest

MAY 22 1994

critics of some of the 1992 and 1993 health reform laws that created the 11 regional Community Health Purchasing Alliances in Florida.

Although some agents such as Edens are warming up to the idea of the alliances, many view them as a threat to their livelihood and an unnecessary layer of bureaucracy mucking up the insurance market.

Some agents are miffed that media attention on the novelty of the alliances has overshadowed other significant insurance reform that exists apart from the alliances. And some agents are suspicious of the discounts touted by the alliances.

"We've had health-insurance reform since 1993," said Marianne King-O'Connor, vice president of employee benefits for James B. Greene & Associates, an Orlando insurance agency.

The voluntary alliances were designed to help small employers exert market pressure on health care through volume purchasing and informed decisions. While it's too early to fairly evaluate the alliances on some of those lofty goals, it's important to note the concerns as the alliance concept is coming under great scrutiny during the congressional debate over health care in Washington.

Edens points out that all policies sold through the alliances must be sold by an agent — a legal requirement that agents successfully lobbied for in Tallahassee.

Edens is one agent who thinks the system is good.

He said Kennedy got a deal that was 26 percent better inside the alliance than it would have been outside the alliance.

The publicity from Kennedy's deal and other anecdotal evidence of great rates has sparked tremendous interest in the business community. The Orlando-based alliance that covers Orange, Brevard, Osceola and Seminole counties has received inquiries from 1,500 businesses.

But Altamonte Springs insurance agent Mike Dwyer thinks the prices inside the alliances often are compared with rates that nobody sells.

Agents vs. alliances

Small businesses don't have to buy insurance through one of the state's Community Health Purchasing Alliances. Even when they do, they still must deal with an insurance agent.

Agents argue that:
■ They sell the same types of policies as alliances, containing the same reforms set by state law.
■ The added costs of operating the alliances ultimately may make their health plans more expensive.
■ The state funds used to operate the alliances are a hidden cost to taxpayers.

Alliances argue that:
■ The volume purchasing power they generate by pooling the business of many small employers is leading to less expensive plans.
■ Employers can offer more than 1 plan to their workers, a feature not available to small businesses outside an alliance.
■ They can produce consumer guides with side-by-side comparisons of all the group health-insurance plans available.

Source: Sentinel research

"You have to be real careful when they give you numbers," said Dwyer, past president of the Central Florida Association of Health Underwriters. "It is 26 percent lower than what? Is it 26 percent lower than a filed rate in Tallahassee that nobody is selling? The prices will eventually come out, and they can be compared with street price to make a real evaluation."

The agents say that many people are unaware that insurance reforms passed with other health-care laws in 1992 and 1993 have made significant changes that have nothing to do with the alliances.

All policies for businesses with 50 or fewer employees are now "guarantee issue," meaning that insurance companies cannot deny coverage for any small business that requests it. Coverage for pre-existing conditions is guaranteed

THE FLORIDA TIMES-UNION

BUSINESS

APR 30 1994

Health alliance ready for members

By Chuck Springston
Business writer

For more than a year, community health purchasing alliances have been something that small businesses could only read about.

But beginning next month, the alliances will be something businesses actually can join

Northeast Florida's community health purchasing alliance, or CHPA (pronounced "chippa"), will begin mailing applications to interested companies this coming week, said Bill Schneider, the alliance's executive director.

The chippa already has received requests for applications, Schneider said. "We have a long list of about 100 in our office."

Businesses that join the chippa in May will likely see coverage take effect June 1, Schneider said.

The chippas, created by the Legislature in April 1993, enable a state's small companies to combine into a group large enough that hospitals, doctors and insurers will typically offer a good price to get those companies' business

For chippa purposes, small businesses are defined as companies with 50 or fewer employees.

Insurers, doctors, hospitals and other health care providers that want to serve the chippas must be part of networks called "accountable health partnerships." Those partnerships compete against each other for the chippa's business.

About 25 to 30 accountable health partnerships submitted their plans and prices to the chippa Feb. 10.

And last week, the chippa signed a contract to have Tampa-based Dun & Bradstreet Plan Services Inc. provide administrative and marketing assistance.

Businesses can call the chippa office in Daytona Beach to get an application And the chippa staff will put the employer's insurance agent in touch with Dun & Bradstreet, which will calculate the premiums manually because the planned computer system is not ready

Businesses interested in the chippa may call its Daytona Beach office at 904-947-3133 until a toll-free line is available in mid-May. After that, they can call 800-4 my CHPA (469-2472).

State's health-care alliances to offer plans to businesses

By Mike Oliver
OF THE SENTINEL STAFF

The health-care seed planted a year ago by Florida lawmakers will begin to bear fruit Monday when regional alliances offer what they promise is affordable health insurance for small businesses.

Whether small businesses consider the insurance a bargain or not won't be apparent right away. But judging from the number of early inquiries logged by the state's 11 regional alliances, interest is high.

The Region 7 alliance, which serves Orange, Seminole, Osceola and Brevard counties, has already heard from 1,000 businesses seeking enrollment information.

As a result, some alliances are asking interested employers to wait a few weeks before looking into the program, unless they're in dire need of health insurance.

"The first two weeks of May, we'll be concentrating on those whose policy is expiring," said

Please see CHPA, C-9

For more information

Membership in a Community Health Purchasing Alliance is available to any Florida business with 50 or fewer employees. Although policies go on sale Monday, alliance officials are asking most businesses to wait a couple of weeks before calling because they already have a backlog of uninsured applicants to process.

Central Florida has been divided among 3 separate alliances. For more information call:

■ (407) 839-0772 in Orange, Seminole, Osceola and Brevard counties.

■ (904) 375-0050 in Lake County.

■ In Volusia County, (800) 452-7929 (Jacksonville).

Alliances aim to drive down costs

CHPA from C-1

Terry McCorvie, executive director of the Orlando-based alliance.

Businesses that have already called can expect to hear back from the alliance in about two weeks, McCorvie said.

"If people get the enrollment information by June 15, they'll be in line for July 1 coverage," he added.

The alliances were created by Florida's 1992 health-care reform law in the hope they would drive down the cost of health insurance by grouping small businesses together and acting as their go-between with insurers.

Membership in an alliance gives an employer access to side-by-side comparisons of various health plans in terms of both coverage and cost.

The Region 7 alliance, for instance, is offering 147 health plans submitted by 34 private insurers and health maintenance organizations.

State health-care officials say plans offered through alliances are less expensive than comparable ones offered in the open market. Some business owners who have previewed the plans have been impressed by the prices and variety.

"So far I'm very impressed," said Roger Olson, president of Contract Resource Associates Inc., a Melbourne business that represents industrial furniture manufacturers. "With the CHPA, we'll spend less money and get better coverage all around."

Health alliances ease burden of small businesses

By CRAIG S. PALOSKY
T une Staff Writer

TAMPA — The state's health reforms may help little Alvin Lynch Jr. stop the bleeding

Alvin, 7, suffers from hemophilia, a blood disorder that turns n or cuts and scrapes into serious wounds Expensive blood-clot-ir_ treatments exhausted the lifetime insurance benefits in his mother's policy last month.

Consignment-shop owner Sabrina Lynch now sees the state's new Cc munity Health Purchasing Alliances, which began offering m l-business insurance this month, as her best hope to get afford-ible insurance for her and Alvin.

"It's guaranteed to be something affordable," said Lynch, who ai , Kid's Worthy Encore in Tampa.

We're a new business, and we don't have a lot of money to put out for health care," she said. "This is one of the best options, other han state aid."

he alliances, created last year under Gov. Lawton Chiles' e h reforms, began marketing health insurance to small business ais month. Their performance should prove the best test yet of Chiles' market-based approach.

oosters contend small businesses could save as much as 40 e ent on health insurance compared to prices outside the allianc-s, helping many pay for insurance for the first time.

"We've got the potential to give them volume, so the rates ac d be competitive," said Cynthia Sampson, executive director of he Brandon-based District 6 alliance.

The state's 11 regional alliances are nonprofit groups, created is year to pool the buying clout of small businesses. They are now a eting dozens of health plans from private insurers that submit-d ids this winter.

Already, at least 500 businesses have sought information about e health plans and rates available in District 6, which serves il orough, Polk, Highlands, Hardee and Manatee counties.

business owners like their options, they could enroll their mployees as early as July 1, Sampson said.

The District 5 alliance, which serves Pinellas and Pasco coun-s has received about 450 inquiries, mostly from self-employed c e and companies with a handful of workers, executive director chard Neiser said.

"They're why we're in business," Neiser said. "They're at a s vantage getting the attention of the insurance companies."

iles traveled to Miami and Titusville Tuesday to honor two of e first businesses to buy insurance through the alliances, including m ure-store owner Kerry Kennedy.

esident Clinton mentioned Kennedy, who laid off his parents c se they cost too much to insure, during a nationally televised

See HEALTH, Page 5

Health alliances ease insurance woes

■ From Page 1

speech on health care in September

Chiles also continues to push to reform the state's medical-welfare programs to help some 1 million people without insurance pay for health coverage. He plans to force lawmakers to tackle the issue next month

Meanwhile, Bay area businesses are investigating their new options through the local alliances.

Mary Martin, who owns a Tampa jewelry shop with her husband, hopes to buy new insurance through the plan. Her store dropped its coverage this month after concluding they paid too much for too little.

"Three hundred dollars per month is not affordable, not for people like us, anyway," Martin said "It's either pay that or pay the mortgage."

Other business owners simply want more complete coverage at a competitive price. For the first time they can go to a single place to review dozens of options

Karen Closner, who owns The Donut Express in Town 'N Country, hopes to find a plan with fewer deductibles than her three-worker restaurant now has.

"It's sort of frustrating," Closner said "When you pay an amount, you expect to have more coverage than just out-of-pocket expenses."

Alliances open on health care

■ The state's plan to control costs starts with lots of questions.

By KIM NORRIS
Times Staff Writer

TAMPA — The phones were ringing steadily Monday at the Hillsborough Community Health Plan Alliance in Tampa.

By 4 p.m., office workers had fielded at least 125 calls from owners of small businesses interested in learning more about the alliances, called chippas, that form the foundation of Florida's ambitious plans to control spiraling health insurance costs and provide coverage to the state's 2.5-million uninsured.

The purpose of the chippas is to pool the collective buying power of small businesses and state agencies to get better health insurance rates. Three-quarters of Florida's uninsured are employees of small businesses and their dependents.

In February, chippas around the state opened bids from insurers interested in participating in the experiment. Since then, the alliances have been compiling the information into comparative rate tables.

On Monday, the state's 11 chippas officially opened for business to sole proprietors and businesses with 50 or fewer employees.

But there were few requests for rate comparisons, according to Cynthia Sampson, executive director of the Tampa chippa, which encompasses Hillsborough, Hardee, Highlands, Manatee and Polk counties. Officials from the Pinellas and Gainesville chippas, which include Pinellas, Pasco, Citrus and Hernando counties, were not available for comment. "The most common questions are 'who are your carriers' and 'what plans do they offer,' " she said.

The Tampa chippa has 31 insurance companies participating. Many of them offer more than one type of plan, such as a health maintenance organization, a preferred provider organization and a straight fee-for-service indemnity plan.

The rates vary widely, but some businesses can realize a savings of as much as 22 percent over rates offered outside the alliance, Sampson said.

Sampson said that if a business has an insurance agent willing to sell the chippa product, the alliance will work through the agent. However, business owners can ask for the rate comparisons directly from the chippa. It is up to the business to purchase the insurance.

Employers with 30 or fewer employees are encouraged to offer at least two different plans to workers, while businesses with 30 to 50 workers are supposed to offer at least three choices. If employees select multiple plans, the employer receives only one enrollment form and one premium bill.

For additional information on chippas and rates, business owners can call their local alliance:

In Hillsborough County, contact the Tampa CHPA at (813) 689-8646

In Citrus and Hernando counties, contact the Gainesville CHPA at (904) 375-0050

In Pasco and Pinellas counties contact the St Petersburg CHPA at (813) 895-7004.

CHPA insurance available

Sun Sentinel 5/1/94

Alliance offering 51 health plans

By LARRY KELLER
Staff Writer

After months of planning, the organization entrusted with arranging affordable health care for workers at small businesses and the self-employed is about to open for business in Broward County.

On Monday, Broward's community health purchasing alliance, called CHPA, will begin providing information on 51 health plans offered by 34 companies and start administering those plans.

But the tens of thousands of Broward workers without health insurance shouldn't get their hopes up soon.

John Erb, executive director of Broward's alliance, said he expects many of the firms that initially buy through the alliance will be bargain hunters that already provide health insurance to workers.

"I don't want the citizens of Broward County to think we have fixed this problem on day one. We haven't," Erb said.

But Erb said he expects companies that don't currently provide health insurance to start signing on as the number of workers in the program grows and rates drop even more.

"This is a beast that's still evolving," Erb said.

Many small businesses know little or nothing about the alliance right now and have made no plans to buy health insurance for workers through it.

"Never heard of it," said Bill Frenzel, owner of Frenzel and Sons Plumbing Co. in Oakland Park. "I wish they would come around here. I'm paying through the nose for insurance."

The state's 11 regional alliances were formed last year as a cornerstone of Florida's Health Care and Insurance Reform Act.

With the federal government debating how to reshape health care on the national level, experts are waiting to see how successful Florida's pioneering program is.

The lofty goal is to provide low-cost quality health care to the estimated 2.7 million Floridians who work for small businesses or are self-employed and have no medical coverage.

In Broward, an estimated 40,000 small businesses employ 201,000 people — many without health insurance — that the alliance hopes to reach.

Erb estimates that the alliance will need 20,000 to 25,000 people subscribing to its health plans before the program pays for itself. That could become critical next year. The alliance is assured of state financing through June 1995.

Sun Sentinel 5/1/94 CHPA

CHPA ready to provide health plans

FROM PAGE 1B

ing carefully and won't likely begin an advertising campaign until this summer. "We're taking a very deliberate approach to our marketing," Erb said.

Eventually, the alliance hopes to win business through a campaign that includes direct mail and newspaper and radio advertisements.

In the meantime, the alliance will continue wooing a group considered crucial to its success: health insurance agents.

"I personally have probably spoken to 500 agents down here," Erb said. "They are our sales force "

The agents must convince small businesses that health insurance through the alliance is a good deal.

"The agents have been very wary of us. They think we're going to be out there selling policies," Erb said.

In fact, the alliance is prohibited from selling insurance.

Still to be determined by the 17-member alliance board is how much to charge small business owners who buy insurance through it. Likely figures are a $20 annual fee plus 70 cents to $1 per employee enrolled, Erb said.

The alliance can arrange health coverage at as much as 20 percent below rates currently paid for comparable plans, Erb said. Rates range greatly — a single man under the age of 30 who doesn't smoke could pay anywhere from $45 to $120 a month.

Despite potential savings to employers, Erb doubts that many small businesses that don't insure their employees will do so through the alliance.

"I don't think that's going to be a substantial number," he said. "Some will never offer their employees insurance. They're just cheap."

Other small business owners simply have too small a profit margin to afford health insurance — even at reduced rates secured by the alliance, Erb said.

If Erb is right, the alliance will fail to significantly help the people it was designed to help. But that will be temporary, he predicts.

"As we enroll more people, the rates get lower," Erb said. "Maybe next year we save 40 percent instead of 20 percent."

Initially, at least, Erb sees more potential sales coming from businesses that already pro-

vide health insurance to their employees, but would like a wider variety of plans or cheaper coverage.

Such as the Grapevine Gourmet Shoppe in Plantation "I've heard of [the alliance], but I don't know the specifics of it," co-owner Paul Frieser said. Frieser began providing health insurance to his dozen full-time employees in January, and is happy with the coverage.

But he is just the sort of businessman Erb thinks may join the alliance, if he can be convinced that comparable health insurance is available at a lower cost.

Frieser said Erb may be right. "I would be foolish not to be interested in looking into it," he said.

Regardless of whom he buys his company's health insurance from, Frieser said it's a good investment. "In order to be competitive, you have to offer health insurance," he said.

Other small business owners may be a tougher sell. Tom Gigler, owner of Nova Plumbing in Oakland Park, hadn't heard of the alliance and doesn't particularly care to learn more about it.

This despite the fact that Gigler is unhappy with the health insurance his employees currently have.

"It's been a nightmare," Gigler said. "As far as I'm concerned, we might as well be shipped to Paraguay and be treated by horse doctors."

But Gigler said he suspects the quality of care available from the alliance's lower-cost plans will be poor. "You get what you pay for," he said. "That's been my experience."

Succinctly summarizing the various plans available through the alliance won't be easy. Allowing for various factors such as the age, gender and marital status of a prospective client, about 10,000 rates are available from the 51 plans, Erb said.

That would be too much information to provide employers, so the alliance will provide comparisons of a couple of common features of each plan. If an employer wants more detailed information, it will be provided, Erb said.

"I have a feeling the number of plans in our CHPA will probably go down over time," Erb said. Those that are not competitively priced will probably get little business and withdraw from the alliance, he said.

"I'd rather have too many than too few," Erb said. "Americans love choice "

ABOUT CHPA

Information about Community Health Purchasing Alliances, called CHPAs (chippas):

Q. What are they?

A. The alliances are local, nonprofit organizations that pool the buying power of small businesses and government to obtain health care for employers with up to 50 full-time workers, the self-employed and eventually, state employees and Medicaid recipients.

Q. Where do they operate?

A. Throughout Florida. Some, as in Broward, cover only one county. Others encompass several counties.

Q. What does a small business or self-employed person get from belonging to a health alliance?

A. By joining other businesses and individuals, members get the same clout as a large employer when bargaining with insurers for health coverage. Alliances will provide members with information on each health care-provider, including prices, enrollee costs, quality, patient satisfaction and specialized coverages. They also will devise a grievance procedure for members who have complaints about their health care provider.

Q. Is participation in a plan mandatory?

A. No, it is voluntary

Q. Will employers contribute to the cost of an employee's premium?

A. Business owners can choose to pay 50 percent, 25 percent or none of the premium charged to their employees. Businesses will pay a fee to belong to an alliance, expected to be a few dollars per employee.

Anybody interested in more information about Broward's community health alliance should telephone the alliance's office at 587-7100

Up to 41% savings possible through local health alliance

By LAURA CASSELS
Daily News Capital Bureau

Small businesses that insure their employees through a new health-purchasing alliance that includes Okaloosa, Santa Rosa and Walton counties could pay up to 41 percent less for health care than other small businesses, alliance officials said last week.

Starting this month, insurance discounts will be available to businesses with 50 or fewer employees through the District 1 Community Health Purchasing Alliance, dubbed CHPA.

CHPA board director Joe Bruner, president of Destin's Big Kahuna's Lost Paradise theme park, said large discounts submitted by insurance companies in February demonstrate managed competition will work.

"Depending on what you choose, you're talking about (up to) 41 percent savings. That's going to raise some eyebrows," Bruner said. "And I think you haven't seen the tip of the iceberg in terms of the savings you'll see in the second year."

The District 1 CHPA comprises Escambia, Santa Rosa, Okaloosa and Walton counties. There are 11 CHPAs statewide.

The mission of the non-profit CHPAS, each supervised by a board of 17 volunteers, most from the private sector, is to recruit small businesses and combine their purchasing power to win lower

ALLIANCE DEALS

State officials took one company in each of the 11 regional alliances to crunch some numbers and illustrate what kinds of deals would be available to alliance members:

Alliance covering Escambia, Santa Rosa, Okaloosa, and Walton counties:
- Current monthly premium in open marketplace: $8,097.04.
- Choice of 91 plans offered through alliance by 19 companies.
- 21 percent average savings for all plans: $1,672.43.

Alliance covering Holmes, Jackson, Washington, Bay, Calhoun, Gadsden, Gulf, Liberty, Franklin, Leon, Wakulla, Jefferson, Madison and Taylor counties:
- Current monthly premium in open marketplace: $7,292.00.
- Choice of 76 plans offered through alliance by 19 companies.
- 24 percent average savings for all plans: $1,769.55.

Please see DEAL/3B

rates from insurance companies.

The grand goal statewide is to bring health-care costs within reach of 2.5 million people who presently are uninsured. Most of those are working people and children. From 1980 to 1990, health-care

Please see ALLIANCE/3B

ALLIANCE

From 1B

costs statewide tripled and they are expected to triple again by the year 2000.

In February, CHPA opened their first bids from insurance companies wanting to do business with the new alliances, created last year under Gov. Lawton Chiles. The bids varied greatly, with the vast majority offering lower prices to CHPA members than on the open market. On average, prices were 25 percent lower.

Deborah Trocki, executive director of the District 1 CHPA, said she found that every company that has called so far could save 15 to 25 percent compared with prices offered outside the CHPA.

The rates are lower partly because CHPAs will take care of enrollments, premium collections and marketing, so insurers avoid those administrative costs.

CUTTING CONFUSION

But the main reasons, according to Bruner and Trocki, are combined purchasing power and forcing insurers to compete item by item, comparing apples with apples.

"We have a third-party administrator to do marketing, billings and administration. So when we told the insurance companies, 'Just tell us what you'll charge for two Tylenols, a hospital room — they went berserk" Bruner said. "They want the thing to be as confusing as possible."

For example, bids in February on the same benefits for a selected Escambia County company with nine employees ranged from $1,400 monthly to $2,000 monthly.

Bruner said that illustrates how well competition in the insurance industry will serve consumers, if they are well-informed. He said complaints about politics being behind health-care reform are bunk.

"What kind of politics is it to say, 'Let's take the lowest bidder'?" Bruner asked.

CHPAs will help cut the confusion by reporting annually on what clients had to say about insurers in their districts, what the costs were, and patient outcomes.

The small-group insurance plans that will be offered in District 1 include:

■ Health-maintenance organizations, or HMOs, which require patients to use providers in the network, except in emergencies, and which generally charge lower premiums.

■ Preferred provider organizations, or PPOs, which pay higher reimbursements when patients choose providers inside their network.

■ Indemnity, or fee-for-service, policies, which let patients choose the provider, but the premiums are generally higher than for other plans.

For nearly all of those plans, the premiums bid by insurance companies in February were lower for CHPA members than for non-members.

Bruner railed against misconceptions about health-care reform, particularly the debate this year in the Legislature over allowing "any willing provider" to serve all patients, which would unravel managed-care plans such as HMOs.

"If you want to go to a rular doctor, pick an indemnity plan or a PPO. If you want a little more choice, pay a little more money," Bruner said, emphasizing that District 2 offers all the options.

"But the guy who works for me who breaks his ankle, he just wants to go to an orthopedic surgeon without it crushing his credit for the rest of his life," said Bruner, who became interested in CHPAs after being unable to find affordable insurance for his own employees.

On the other hand, some doctors argue that in HMOs, they feel pressured to do fewer tests and procedures, to cut costs, while feeling compelled to do the procedures, partly to protect themselves from lawsuits.

That debate, and one about letting poor people now insured by Medicaid join CHPAs and pay part of their own premiums, likely will be settled when the Legislature meets in a special session on health care a month from now.

OPEN FOR BUSINESS

Meanwhile, CHPAs are eager to get to business.

Statewide, businesses that join a CHPA and have 30 or fewer employees would offer at least two plans to employees. Larger businesses would offer at least three Self-employed , people also can join.

Employers who enroll in a CHPA would pay half the cost for their employees' coverage, but there is no mandate that they join.

The idea is that lower-cost insurance would help many small businesses that want insurance for their work force but cannot afford it at present rates or cannot get it because one or more of their employees would not qualify.

"It was the working- middle class that could not afford health care before, unless they went to the emergency room," said Sue Rushing, owner of Kirby Rushing home builders in DeFuniak Springs and a District 1 CHPA board member.

"If they went to the emergency room, maybe they couldn't pay for it. Then, you and I paid for it."

Another advantage of coverage through a CHPA is that no one can be denied coverage. Rates will be based on only five "community rating" factors: county of residence, gender, age, family composition, and whether the insured smokes. Generally, pre-existing conditions will not be considered.

The District 1 CHPA will provide enrollment information starting next week and will officially open for business May 11 at an open house in Pensacola.

A town meeting for Okaloosa and Walton county enrollments is scheduled at Okaloosa-Walton Community College on May 18 from 7 to 9 p.m.

A similar meeting is being set for Santa Rosa County on May 23 or May 24, Trocki said.

Annual membership fees are $25 for member groups, plus $4 monthly per insured employee Fees for associate members, who receive the annual performance reports with which to do their own insurance shopping, are $250 a year.

For more information, call (800) 469-2472) or the District 1 CHPA office in Pensacola at (904) 477-7666.

TROPICOOL

A calendar for Tropicool and other events for the month of May.
Page 1E

SUMMER TRAVEL

Balloons in New Jersey, Goombay in Florida ... Interesting things are happening all over the country.
Page 1D

HEAT LOSE

Hawks even series 1 1.
Page 1C

SUNDAY

Naples Daily News

Collier County's newspaper

Sunday, May 1, 1994

$1.25 a

Small-business owners enter new era of health care

Regional alliances open Monday

Daily News staff and wire reports

Small-business owners in Collier and Lee counties will find themselves on the cutting edge of health-care reform Monday when Florida's brave new world of managed competition opens for business.

Starting Monday, owners of businesses with 50 or fewer employers will be able to enroll in one of 11 health-care alliances across Florida — the first in the country to have a statewide network of insurance alliances.

The idea is that, by joining together the small firms can reap the benefits of volume purchasing enjoyed by big businesses That's one of the central concepts of the health-care reform model known as managed competition.

State lawmakers created the non-profit, private Community Health Purchasing Alliances a year ago. Although they are state-chartered, the CHPAS (pronounced "chippas") are run by 17-member boards appointed last fall by Gov. Lawton Chiles and legislative leaders.

Membership is voluntary and open to self-employed people and businesses with up to 50 workers. The Southwest Florida CHPA includes Collier, Lee, Charlotte, Hendry, DeSoto, Glades and Sarasota counties.

The alliances can't purchase or negotiate on behalf of their members. They have to offer all plans submitted by insurance companies and health maintenance organizations.

But the alliances can provide their members with the data to compare one plan to another. Much of their work will be handled by outside benefits management companies hired this

See REFORM, Page 12A

Reform:
Alliances
begin Monday

Continued from 1A

spring

"You can walk through the door (Monday), get the comparative rates and begin shopping," said Doug Cook, director of the Agency for Health Care Administration.

The coverage purchased by alliance members will take effect in June.

Two-thirds of the plans submitted to the alliances had cheaper premiums than plans available in the open market. Cook said. The average drop in price was .25 percent.

"That seems to me to be a good deal," he said.

As well as lower costs, the plans offer patient choice. Cook said. Only 20 percent were closed networks like HMOs. The rest were either traditional fee-for-service indemnity plans or preferred provider organizations, which have open networks that patients can leave if they pay a higher price.

Some 50 insurers offered more than 1,300 health plans, with an average of 100 plans in each of the 11 alliance districts.

In Southwest Florida, companies — marriages of insurance firms with hospitals and doctors — have developed more than 100 medical plans for businesses who join the CHPA.

Bidding companies were asked to submit bids for an eight-employee company and a 25-employee company, both of which have specific demographics.

For Collier County, hospital giant Humana Corp., which plans to form an HMO in Collier, offered initial low bids of $643.77 per month for the eight-employee company and $2,125.75 per month for the 25-employee company.

The highest initial bid for Collier came from the CIGNA Corp., which offered a $1,791-per-month plan for the eight-employee company and a $6,414-per-month plan for the 25-employee organization.

Across the state, the directors and board members of the alliances aren't sure what they're going to be faced with when they open for business Monday. Many hope for a low-key, quiet beginning to give them time to work out any kinks before they publicize a grand opening in the middle of the month.

"We're designing the road as we're building it and we want to make sure the first day we open it we don't have bumper-to-bumper traffic," said Terry McCorvie, executive director of the alliance that includes Orange, Osceola, Seminole and Brevard counties.

In Hialeah, Lynn Kislak, chairwoman of the alliance that includes Dade and Monroe counties, said alliance officials are excited about opening.

"There's this great sense of anticipation," she said.

Regional health care alliances are ready to do business

Associated Press

TALLAHASSEE ... Kerry Kennedy doesn't have any expertise in health care reform.

He's just another small business man who wants to provide medical care to his workers and has looked all over for coverage that doesn't bankrupt him.

Kennedy got a sneak peek last week into Florida's brave new world of managed competition, which is for business Monday.

"Im, man, I am very impressed," said, "I had no idea going into this thing what it would entail."

The executive director of one of Florida's regional health care alliances met with Kennedy and his insurance agent to review the menu of plans that will be available in three regions.

Kennedy, who owns a Titusville furniture store, found himself in the spotlight Friday when his new health alliances would make much difference in the medical insurance market.

But after the meeting, he marveled at how many choices of affordable plans were available through the alliance. "This is definitely a change," he said.

Starting Monday, Kennedy and other small-business employers will be able to enroll in one of 11 health care alliances across Florida.

The idea is that, by joining together, the small businesses can reap the benefits of volume purchasing already enjoyed by big businesses. That's one of the central concepts of the health care reform model known as managed competition.

The Community Health Purchasing Alliances were created by state lawmakers a year ago.

They're non-profit, private entities — state chartered, but run by 17-member boards appointed last fall by Gov. Lawton Chiles and legislative leaders.

Membership is voluntary and open to self-employed people and businesses with up to 50 workers.

The alliances can't purchase or negotiate on behalf of their members. They have to offer all plans submitted by insurance companies and health maintenance organizations.

But the alliances can provide their members with the data to compare one plan to another. Much of their work will be handled by outside benefits management companies hired for the job.

"You can walk through the door ...

Two-thirds of the plans submitted to the alliances had cheaper premiums than plans available in the open market, said Cook. The average drop in price was 25 percent.

"That seems to me to be a good deal," he said.

Ft. Myers News Press
May!

Kennedy had been hesitant to get his hopes up that Florida's new health alliances would make much difference in the medical insurance market.

"I'm not a health person I'm not an insurance agent," Kennedy said. "I'm a furniture man."

New world of health insurance alliances to begin

The future of managed competition for health care begins Monday in Florida.

By JACKIE HALIFAX
of The Associated Press

TALLAHASSEE — Kerry Kennedy doesn't have any expertise in health care reform.

He's just another small business owner who wants to provide medical benefits to his workers and who has looked all over for coverage that didn't bankrupt him.

Kennedy got a sneak peek last week into Florida's brave new world of managed competition, which opens for business Monday.

"Oh, man. I am very impressed," he said. "I had no idea going into this meeting what it would entail."

The executive director of one of Florida's new regional health care alliances met with Kennedy and his insurance agent to review the insurance plans that would be available to small employers who join the alliances.

Kennedy, who owns a Titusville furniture store, found himself in the national spotlight last fall when his health care woes were described by President Clinton in his State of the Union address to Congress.

Kennedy had been hesitant about getting his hopes up that Florida's new health alliances would make much difference in the medical insurance market.

"I'm not a health care person. I'm not an insurance agent," Kennedy said. "I'm a furniture man."

But after the meeting, he marveled at how many kinds of affordable plans were available through the alliances. "This is definitely a change," he said.

Starting Monday, Kennedy and other small business owners will be able to enroll in one of 11 health care alliances across Florida.

The idea is that, by joining together, the small businesses can reap the benefits of volume purchasing already enjoyed by big businesses That's one of the central concepts of the health care reform model known as managed competition.

The Community Health Purchasing Alliances were created by state lawmakers a year ago.

They're non-profit, private entities. Although they are state chartered, they are run by 17-member boards appointed last fall by Gov. Lawton Chiles and legislative leaders

Membership is voluntary and open to self-employed people and businesses with up to 50 workers.

The alliances can't purchase or negotiate on behalf of their members. They have to offer all plans submitted by insurance companies and health maintenance organizations.

But the alliances can provide their members with the data to compare one plan to another. Much of their work will be handled by outside benefits management companies hired this spring.

"You can walk through the door (Monday), get the comparative rates and begin shopping," said Doug Cook, director of the Agency for Health Care Administration.

Two thirds of the plans submitted to the alliances had cheaper premiums than plans available in the open market, said Cook. The average drop in price was 25 percent.

"That seems to me to be a good deal," he said.

As well as wet costs, the plans offer patient choice, Cook said. Only 20 are were closed networks like HMOs. The rest are either traditional fee for service i.e. only plans or preferred provider organizations, which have open networks but patients can leave if they pay a higher price.

Some 50 insurers offered more than 1,300 health plans, with an average of 100 plans in each of the 11 alliance districts.

The coverage purchased by alliance members won't take effect until June.

Florida's health care alliances drawing attention

Jackie Hallifax
The Associated Press

TALLAHASSEE. — Small business owners aren't the only ones interested in the performance of the regional health care purchasing alliances that open for business

Experts and pros from Washington to New Jersey to Wyoming are following the fate of Florida's version of managed competition as the debate over national health care reform continues.

"Florida's a very important model," said Nancy Barrand, a senior program officer with the Robert Wood Johnson Foundation in Princeton, NJ.

Florida is the first state to have a statewide network of insurance alliances, Barrand said.

But several states have approved creating some form of purchasing alliance or cooperative, said Erin Haugh, a senior policy analyst for the Health Policy

ances run by boards appointed by the governor and legislative leaders. The alliances are open to small business and enrollment begins Monday.

"The whole thing depends on how well you execute," Dr. Paul Ellwood, president of the Jackson Hole Group said. "The idea is right."

California has a single alliance with six geographic regions. Since last July, more than 50,000 people have enrolled. Rates dropped 6 percent this year, following a 15 percent drop last year.

"They've been very, very successful," Haugh said.

Florida, however, is the first to have a network of 11 state-chartered nonprofit private alli-

other states.

"The thing that's special about Florida is you cover the whole state," he said.

Haugh said Minnesota also has had alliances up and running for about a year and Texas is on the verge of launching state-chartered alliances in half the state.

In Washington state, cooperatives approved last year are scheduled to begin operating in mid-1995.

Other states that have passed laws calling for some version of health purchasing alliances include Iowa, North Carolina, South Carolina, Kentucky and Ohio, Haugh said.

Institute, a private organization in Washington.

"California was actually the first state to open its doors and start enrolling people," Haugh said. "It's also the first one, that was somehow state-sanctioned."

Florida, however, is the first to have a network of 11 state-chartered nonprofit private alliances. Ellwood said Florida's efforts are important work is different in scale from the

ALLIANCES: Most premiums were lower for CHPA members

From Page 1D

ployees ranged from more than $9,000 monthly to slightly more than $5,000 monthly

"What does that tell you about the fragmentation of small-group coverage?" Jones said, suggesting that the complexity of insurance policies makes it hard for consumers to compare them and choose the best quality at the best price.

The CHPAs will do those comparisons for their members, he said, and will report annually on what clients had to say about insurers, what the costs were, and the patient outcomes.

The small-group insurance plans that will be offered in District 2 include:

■ Health-maintenance organizations, or HMOs, which require patients to use providers in the network, except in emergencies, and which generally charge lower premiums;

■ Preferred provider organizations, or PPOs, which pay higher reimbursements when patients choose providers inside their network and,

■ Indemnity, or fee-for-service, policies, which let patients choose the provider, but the premiums are generally higher than for other plans.

For nearly all of those plans, the premiums bid by insurance companies in February were lower for CHPA members than for non-members

However, the range of choices varies from county to county, with rural counties at the west end of the district having the fewest options.

For instance, while four of District 2's 18 bidders agreed to offer HMO plans in Leon County, only two offered HMOs in Bay County and none offered them in Bay's neighboring rural counties.

"In terms of HMOs and PPOs, we have a very undeveloped managed-care district," Jones said "Unfortunately, there's not a great number of choices in the rural areas."

Barr and Jones said they hope that will change in the next few years.

"We've had three carriers who have said, 'We see the CHPA process as a vehicle to increase our market share,' which means doing more business," Jones said.

Meanwhile, he said, the rural counties at least have more options than they had before, and lower prices than before.

Statewide businesses that join a CHPA and have 30 or fewer employees would offer at least two plans to their employees; larger businesses would offer at least three. Self-employed people also could

---

Annual membership fees are $25 for member groups of 25 or fewer employees, and $50 for larger groups, plus $4 monthly per insured employee Fees for associate members, who receive the annual performance reports with which to do their own insurance shopping, are $100 a year.

---

for their employees' coverage, but there is no mandate that they join.

Jones said lower-cost insurance should help many small businesses that want insurance for their workers, but cannot afford it at present rates or cannot get it because one or more of their employees would not qualify. He and others predicted greater savings and more choices in future years.

Jones and others said the advantages of CHPA insurance are not limited to discounted premiums For instance, no one in the CHPA can be denied coverage. Rates will be based on only five "community rating" factors: county of residence, gender, age, family composition, and whether the insured smokes. Generally, pre-existing conditions will not be considered.

Meanwhile, CHPA officials are watching with interest to see whether the Legislature adopts the governor's Health Security Act during a special session a month from now. That plan would allow many poor, working people now insured by Medicaid — but who could pay their premiums with state help — to join CHPAs, further boosting their purchasing clout.

The District 2 CHPA will provide enrollment information starting next week. However, Jones and Barr said complete, detailed information on all the plans to be offered in District 2 won't be available until mid-month or early June.

Annual membership fees are $25 for member groups of 25 or fewer employees, and $50 for larger groups, plus $4 monthly per insured employee. Fees for associate members, who receive the annual performance reports with which to do their own insurance shopping, are $100 a year.

More information...

Cut-rate insurance arrives

Starting Monday, Community Health Purchasing Alliances will offer health insurance plans to businesses with fewer than 50 employees.

DAVID COX
Herald Capitol Bureau

TALLAHASSEE — Big business buying power for health insurance becomes available for small businesses and the self-employed in Florida beginning Monday

That's when Florida's 11 Community Health Purchasing Alliances, or CHPAs, start offering health insurance plans to businesses with fewer than 50 employees

The alliances are the cornerstone of the health care reform act Gov. Lawton Chiles pushed through the Legislature last year. They pool the money of thousands of small businesses to buy health insurance plans at volume discounts — like big businesses already do.

More than 26,000 small businesses in Manatee County qualify to buy health insurance through CHPA, said Cynthia Sampson, executive director for the District 6 CHPA, which is headquartered in Brandon.

About 300 businesses in the district, including about 20 in Manatee County, already expressed interest in joining the CHPA

District 6 includes Manatee, Hillsborough, Polk, Hardee and Highlands counties

Sarasota County is in a CHPA district with DeSoto, Charlotte, Glades, Lee, Hendry and Collier counties.

Statewide, 306,000 small businesses qualify for membership in CHPAs and 45 percent of them do

not now provide health insurance for their employees, said Ed Towey, spokesman for the Agency for Health Care Administration.

"Anybody who wants to sign up and buy (beginning Monday), they can," Towey said Friday

Companies now providing health insurance to workers can shop the CHPA for a better deal.

Michael Bennett, president of Aladdin Ward Electric and Air in Bradenton, said the program probably will help most those businesses with 15 or fewer employees or small firms that have trouble getting insurance because an employee or two have existing health problems.

Under the state law, insurance companies offering plans through CHPA cannot deny insurance to a company because employees have existing health problems. Rates are affected only by age, sex, the county in which an employee lives, the number of persons in his or her family and whether family members use tobacco products.

"It will help small businesses where one of the people in the group has a pre-existing condition that nobody wants to write a policy for because of that one person," said Bennett, who is a member of the District 6 CHPA board.

However, the alliances aren't the cure-all for health insurance, Bennett said, because the plans are voluntary and don't include workers' compensation insurance Unless the plans are mandatory for all businesses, he said, many businesses that offer insurance cannot compete with others that offer higher wages but no health coverage.

Chiles wanted to make the plans mandatory for all Florida businesses, but the Legislature weakened the provision to voluntary status.

So far in District 6, 31 groups of hospitals, doctors and managed care facilities (such as health maintenance organizations) have offered 48 types of health insurance plans for sale through the CHPA, Sampson said.

In a recent comparison of two types of businesses in District 6, the Agency for Health Care Administration determined the CHPA can save them a bundle.

For example, a business providing coverage for 52 employees plus their families — and paying $117,096 a year for insurance could save $4,152 to $59,460 in premiums, depending on the plan selected.

61

Bradenton Herald, Sunday, May 1, 1994

In another example, CHPA could save a company insuring 11 persons — seven employees and four dependents — and now paying $16,620 a year for insurance anywhere from $96 to $7,644 in premiums.

The local CHPA will begin selling policies Monday, Sampson said Actual coverage won't begin until 30.45 days after a plan is purchased.

Some CHPAs will not start selling policies for a couple weeks after the official start-up Monday, said Towey, the health care agency spokesman.

Chiles is scheduled to swing through the state the week of May 16 to officially mark the opening of all CHPAs.

Health alliance rates ready, agents can begin to sell

By STEPHANIE L. JACKSON
Palm Beach Post Staff Writer

The prices are in. After months of hearing about the Community Health Purchasing Alliance formed under state health-care reform, small businesses can now find out how much insurance coverage in the alliance will cost.

Insurance agents will be able to sell it.

The final rates for Palm Beach, Martin, Okeechobee, St. Lucie and Indian River counties came in Monday. A few agents and brokers received a nearly complete list of rates on Friday.

Bruce Silver, president of a West Palm Beach insurance consulting firm called Silver Financial Network, said he had compared the rates inside and outside the alliance and was already lining up clients to join the alliance.

"These rates are very aggressive," he said Monday. "With certain businesses, I could not get them these rates outside. And other clients, I'm going to be able to save thousands."

Silver serves on the technical advisory committee for the alliance, which is one of 11 state-supported, nonprofit organizations formed last

Please see ALLIANCES/4B

GETTING COVERED

■ **BUSINESSES WITH 1 TO 50 EMPLOYEES** are eligible for membership in the Community Health Purchasing Alliance, or CHPA. The alliance was formed to allow small businesses to pool purchases and lower insurance costs.

■ **TWO BENEFITS PACKAGES** are available — basic and standard. Both cover maternity. The basic package covers less and requires larger copayments.

■ **RATES VARY** according to five factors — the employee's age, sex, county of residence, tobacco use and inclusion of a spouse or children. (Health problems may not be considered.) For example, monthly premiums for a Palm Beach County woman, 50, with standard benefits range from $128 to $356 for an HMO, from $153 to $490 for a PPO (Preferred Provider Organization) and from $218 to $475 for an indemnity plan.

■ **FOR MORE INFORMATION,** call (800) 4MY-CHPA from 8 a.m to 6 p.m Monday through Friday.

Carriers offer 20-25% savings

ALLIANCES
From 1B

year to pool insurance buyers. The alliances were designed to lower costs.

Silver said some carriers are offering savings of up to 20 and 25 percent, especially for young men.

"There's no way I know of for an employer to purchase an HMO plan for a male under 30 for less than $60 a month" outside the alliance, he said.

Through the alliance, a single Palm Beach County man in his 20s could be enrolled for standard HMO coverage with Prudential for $47.52, Humana for $50.80 and Blue Cross/Blue Shield for $60.08. Those rates do not include alliance fees of $4 per employee per month and $25 annually for the company.

"There is a great variation among the carriers. Overall, I think the rates look good," said Marjorie Silberman, the alliance's executive director.

The alliance won't sell the insurance — interested agents will. About 225 agents attended a training session last week, she said.

Rates are now available on paper, but Dun & Bradstreet plans to offer "customized" rate quotes in several weeks.

THE DAYTONA BEACH SUNDAY NEWS-JOURNAL, May 29, 1994

Legislature should back managed competition

THE EDITORIAL

Doctors' groups lobbied hard for amendments that could wipe out the ability of HMOs to act as medical gatekeepers.

The biggest chunk of unfinished business left from this year's regular session of the Florida Legislature is health care.

Last week, Gov. Lawton Chiles called a special session beginning June 7 to give the legislators another crack at it. Unfortunately, it's still unclear whether two tries will be enough.

During the regular session, the health-care package bogged down on eligibility for state-subsidized health-care plans and regulation of health maintenance organizations.

The eligibility debate settled on familiar partisan lines. Democrats wanted more people covered; Republicans wanted to restrict coverage to the very poor.

THE HMO DEBATE, however, broke down on less familiar lines: HMOs and insurers vs. doctors.

Many medical specialists feel their businesses are threatened by the limits HMOs place on patients. Doctors' groups lobbied hard for amendments that could wipe out the ability of HMOs to act as medical gatekeepers.

One of these proposals was dubbed "any willing provider." Under that proposal, HMOs and similar organizations would be forced to pay for procedures done by any physician as long as that physician agrees to meet an HMO's price.

This would destroy much of the advantage HMOs have in contracting for medical services. It would guarantee higher medical costs.

A similar proposal is "direct access," which means an HMO would have to pay for a specialist's services without the patient first being referred by a primary care doctor.

In other words, if you have a headache, you would be free to go to a neurologist without first checking in with a general practitioner. As with the any-willing-provider proposal, this would undermine the ability of HMOs to watch over costs.

Taken together, these proposals would doom any health-care reform based on managed competition and send health-care costs soaring.

Medical special interests are certain to bring these proposals back to the legislature. They need to be defeated.

AS IF the issues debated in the special session were not complex enough, a new matter was introduced when the governor signed a tobacco liability measure into law.

The law allows Florida to sue tobacco companies to recover the costs of treating Medicaid patients suffering from smoking-related diseases. Those costs are estimated at $1.2 billion since 1989.

Some business leaders, however, fear the law could be used to sue other companies on similar grounds. This appears very unlikely.

Nevertheless, the Legislature will consider a proposal during the special session to limit the law to the tobacco industry. And the tobacco lobby will make every effort to overturn the law.

The issues are difficult and the lobbying is going to be intense. All off which promises to make the second week in June a very difficult one in Tallahassee.

FLORIDA TODAY, Monday May 23 1994 .

Health-care alliances help small companies

Brevard County earned another footnote in history books when Titusville businessman Kerry Kennedy was recognized recently as the first Florida employer enrolled in a community health-purchasing alliance.

Other small businesses need to follow Kennedy's example and sign up for the purchasing alliances, which are key elements in President Clinton's health-reform plan.

The state Legislature established 11 purchasing alliances in Florida in 1993 to allow small businesses to voluntarily pool their buying power, making insurance more affordable to them.

To qualify, businesses must have no more than 50 employees, and at least 70 percent of those workers must be provided with health insurance either from an alliance or some other source.

The basic benefits packages were set up by the state, but rates vary according to the company and plan selected.

Kennedy's business problems caused by rising health care costs were mentioned by Clinton during a September 1993 speech unveiling the president's health-reform proposals.

> ## To learn more
>
> To find out more about community health purchasing alliances, call 1-800-469-2472.

Gov. Lawton Chiles flew to Titusville last Tuesday to hand Kennedy two new insurance policies purchased through the state alliance.

Kennedy's old plan provided only hospital coverage for him and three employees.

For a slightly higher premium, the alliance-provided plan has comprehensive medical coverage with a $500 deductible.

"It's a very attractive plan," Kennedy said. "It's providing affordable health care coverage, which is great for me as an employer."

Some insurance agents are wary of the new system, which they see as a threat to their industry, although employers still must go through agents to purchase policies through an alliance.

That skepticism is understandable, but the alliances deserve a chance.

With about 2.5 million Floridians — about one in five — lacking health insurance and many others underinsured, it's time to find new ways to address this problem.

Small businesses in Florida need to take advantage of the purchasing alliances so affordable health insurance will be available to as many workers as possible.

Businesses look to insurance group for relief

By CATHY CUMMINS
Tribune Staff Writer

INVERNESS — Monthly health-care premiums of up to $500 per employee forced the Inverness Regional Eye Care Center to look for a new insurance company earlier this year.

The business found lower rates through Blue Cross and Blue Shield, but says business manager Jo Holdaway, "We're still looking."

Area insurance agents met Thursday to learn about plans offered under the Region 3 Community Health Purchasing Alliance. The alliance was formed to help small businesses like the the eye care center and its 12 employees, said Executive Director Jim Sullivan

The region has 16 counties and stretches from Hernando on the south to Hamilton and Columbia in the north, said Michelle Sutton, who runs the Region 3 office in Gainesville.

In Citrus County, 17 insurance plans are being offered, Sullivan said. Some of the companies have well-known names, such as Blue Cross and Blue Shield, while others are smaller, he said.

The plans offered through the alliance range from a traditional 80-20 split on doctors' bills to an HMO arrangement, Sutton said.

The goal is to bring down the cost of insurance by grouping small companies to increase their buying power, Sullivan said.

"Some [plans] are real bargains compared to what was on the market before. Others are pretty small arto what's out there now," he said.

More than 700 businesses in the 17-county region have asked for information about the alliance, he said.

"Small businesses will have the same advantage as big

See INSURANCE, Page 5

The Tampa Tribune, Friday, June 3, 1994

Insurance alliance may provide affordable rates

■ From Page 1

businesses," said Betsy Latliff, one of 17 agents on the Region 3 alliance board.

The alli ances were created last year under Gov. Lawton Chiles' health reforms. They began marketing health insurance to small business this month. Supporters of the plan say small businesses could save as much as 40 percent on health insurance compared to prices outside the alliances. Some companies will be able to afford insurance for their employees for the first time.

Their rates appeal to Holdaway, who piped the alliance telephone number from a newspaper article months ago during her search for her health-care rates.

"We all will have to have health care and we all are paying for the uninsured right now," Latliff said. "It's just cost shifting. [Under the alliance] you'll be insured, just a different way."

Information about the Region 3 alliance is available by calling 1-800-469-2472

TAMPA TRIBUNE

Health-care alliance patient with clients

By STEPHEN SMITH
Herald Staff Writer

They're motivated sellers, but the people running Broward's health purchasing cooperative don't want to sell too much, too soon. They got their wish in the first month of brokering health-insurance plans.

Sales total so far one

The phone jangles relentlessly at the headquarters of the Community Health Purchasing Alliance, staffers peppered with questions from small-business owners and workers More than 1,000 calls in one month They're hoping cautious callers will turn into motivated buyers.

"In my business, the worst thing I can ever do is get someone in the door and not be able to service them properly," said alliance board member Keith Koenig, an executive at Waterbed City. "They'd be more mad at me than ever."

But if you had to choose just one customer, you would probably pick Howard S. Miller, consummate satisfied customer. He's a Hollywood lawyer with a modest practice.

And, after May 31, he was going to be a man without health insurance. Miller figured it wouldn't be easy to find a good policy at a fair rate — he suffers from rheumatoid arthritis, and many health plans don't want to sell to people who already have medical problems

That's when he called the fledgling purchasing alliance. He harvested some information about rates and benefits, called an insurance agent he knows and, by June 1, had a new policy. It provides coverage at least as good as what he used to have.

And it's cheaper. His old policy cost about $800 a month to cover

PLEASE SEE ALLIANCE, 29R

Health purchasing alliance not pressuring customers

ALLIANCE, FROM 18R

Miller and his daughter. Now he pays about $350 a month to belong to a Blue Cross and Blue Shield of Florida health plan.

The health alliance was created by the Legislature to help small businesses get medical insurance for their workers — insurance now priced beyond the bottom lines of many small companies.

The buying cooperative embraces the ethos of strength in numbers. By pooling the resources of hundreds of companies and thousands of workers, the alliance is supposed to get a better deal for workers who can barely afford insurance now.

"What more could I ask for?" Miller said. "They offered me a plan from a major insurer at a reasonable cost without looking at pre-existing conditions."

When will somebody else buy a policy through the alliance? A full-scale sales job won't start until later in the summer — and some think that's too long.

"Why are we waiting until

August?" said alliance board member Preston Henn. "You've got to move."

Sales are slow across the state, but the architects of the system expected that in the early days, as companies do their balancing act

"You've got a lot of people who are in the process of buying and making their buying decision," said Ed Towey, spokesman for the state Agency for Health Care Administration.

"What's more interesting is the people knocking on the door wanting information. Sure, it would be nice to have billions of people already, but this all takes time. You've got to have patience."

LEARN MORE

For more information about Broward's Community Health Purchasing Alliance, call 587-7108 between 9 a.m. and 5 p.m. Monday through Friday.

Employer believer in CHPA

Lee: Health plan quiet revolution

Alliance questions, answers/4A

Linda Zettler
ws Journal

James Lee isn't officially responsible for spreading the word about Community Health Purchasing Alliances — but he wants to The health insurance system for small businesses slashed his employees' rates almost in

"Nobody knows about it. This is almost a solution. And the people who are hearing about it don't understand it," Lee said.

Lee, a Loss of three, has attended every meeting of the board that made it happen. He even bought newspaper ads at his own expense to advertise the service to other small business owners.

WHAT'S A CHPA?
Community Health Purchasing Alliances are locally controlled groups that provide comparisons of health insurance plans for businesses with 50 and fewer employees. Details: 1-800-469-2472 weekdays between 7 a.m. and 4 p.m.

Lee Insurance Agency was one of the first two businesses to sign up with the Community Health Purchasing Alliance for District 1, which covers Escambia, Santa Rosa, Okaloosa and Walton counties. In May, 11 CHPAs (called "chip-pas") throughout Florida began acting as comparison shoppers for small businesses that crave the power of bulk-buying for health insurance.

Under the old plan for Lee's agency, he paid $438 a month to get $500-deductible insurance plans for himself and two employees. The other employee, vice president Dale Buck, had insurance through his wife's job at $362 a month for him and his two daughters. Together the employees were paying $1,064.56 for their insurance needs.

When Lee joined CHPA, staff members got plans with $250 deductibles and added Buck and his two daughters. Their total is now $608.85 — a 43 percent savings.

Lee, who pays 100 percent of his employees'

See HEALTH, 5A

James Lee, owner of a small insurance agency, holds one of his company's CHPA certificates. The new program helps small companies like Lee's offer health insurance to employees at a saving.

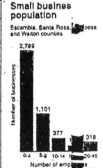

Health plan 'almost a revolution'

FROM 1A

premiums, is saving $178.64 a month, although he s covering an additional employee and offering broader plans

Hostick and his family, who saw a $150 difference in his premiums, are actually saving $260.06 a month because Lee is picking up Hostick's tab.

"I'm having a difficult time finding a downside," Lee said.

An agent who usually deals with property and casualty insurance, Lee is shifting his agency's business to focus more on health since CHPA came along. Ten different businesses have contacted him about CHPA plans because they'd heard him talk of his experience through the media. He enrolled them all, saving each from 16 percent to 40 percent.

"CHPA recreated the system and did it in such a way that we have decided to get more heavily involved," Lee said. "Certainly, I'm in the business of writing insurance and getting paid for it, but I've got 2,500 policies in effect already. And adding a few more doesn't change the total very much. The profit is a small part of my enthusiasm."

Leading the way

Florida is ahead in the race to reform health care, Lee and others believe.

For a couple of debate-intensive years, the federal government has wrestled with revamping a health-care system that costs Americans a bigger chunk of its gross national product than any other country in the world while millions go uninsured.

In Florida, Gov. Lawton Chiles has pushed his own agenda, resulting in the Health Reform Act of 1993 through which CHPAs were born.

The alliances were set up to help businesses with 50 or fewer employees find affordable health insurance. In District 1, 4,749 licensed small businesses are eligible to join, and that doesn't count the self-employed.

"I think it's going to be overwhelmingly successful once the public hears about it. We haven't gotten enough press yet," said Deborah A. Trocki, District 1 CHPA's executive director, who has been speaking to up to three groups a day.

Advertising through the local alliance and through the "third part administrator" will pick up Dun & Bradstreet Plan Services of Tampa coordinates the process through which employers, agents and insurance carriers in eight districts use the system. It's the agency callers reach when phoning CHPA's 800-number.

How it works

The local alliances are governed by boards of 17 people from their districts 11 business representatives, three consumers and three government officials.

The CHPA's main function so far has been gathering bids on insurance policies, which have been compiled into one book for small business owners to peruse. It's the ultimate in comparison shopping, Lee said.

Price bids on basic and standard plans in District 1 came back from 17 major carriers, offering traditional deductible-type plans along with the newer maintenance-driven programs. In all, 80 combinations exist, Lee said.

The rates, which carriers can adjust quarterly, may be based only on age, sex, county of residence, number of family members and tobacco use.

For many people, this solves the problem of being unable to get insurance because of a pre-existing condition. CHPA requires only a waiting period depending on past coverage.

"The whole idea is to untie an individual employee's insurance from his employment," Lee said. "You're all in the same boat so you can move around."

Businesses join the alliance for $25 a year and then can allow employees to enroll in the plans they choose. If the business has fewer than 30 employees, it must offer at least two plans; if 30 or more employees, at least three.

Participation is voluntary. But once employers commit, they are expected to contribute toward employees' plans — generally at least half of the lowest monthly individual employee rate available among the plans the business offers.

The employee pays the rest. Businesses always write only one check — to CHPA. Prices are guaranteed for a year.

Feeling the effects

Trocki expects the alliances to initially offer health insurance but who want to lock in lower costs for a year.

But organizers also hope to draw those without insurance. Some people like J.D. Robinson soon will re-enter the world of the insured through CHPA.

A salesman at Merchants Paper Co., Robinson has been without coverage for more than a year since he left college and his parents' plan. "(It's been) a big-time worry. I have bad ankles. . . Every time I turn my ankle and it swells up, I don't know if it's broken. But I can't afford to go get X-rays every time."

After getting recent quotes of $160 a month, Robinson, 21, will pay about $24 a month for his plan, which starts July 1. His employer splits the cost.

"It's going to help us out especially me and him," said Robinson, referring to a co-worker who's still paying off medical treatment he had to charge on Visa.

Though the CHPA offers plans that range from 16 to 40 percent savings, Trocki said, those hardest to reach will be businesses with up to four employees, limited capital and low profits.

The program's biggest drawback impacts the insurance industry. Trocki said Agents and carriers must learn a new way of doing business.

"The insurance carriers will no longer be able to cherry-pick," Trocki said. "They're concerned that they'll be more work. But (the set up) certainly been the downside for the public years."

And though businesses select CHPA plans with a help many agents worry they'll be phased out of the process. Consumers then would lose the one personal link they have to make certain plans and care are tailored to them, said Pat Scherf, an independent agent who specializes in group health insurance.

"I'm concerned," said Scherf, who worries about what CHPAs will evolve into. "I believe agents and brokers may not be in the small group business two or three years."

Lee, who teaches a property and casualty insurance class Pensacola Junior College, said that about a third of his 40 to 60 students in the last two years have been health insurance agents who were coming back to learn additional area.

Growing curiosity

While local coordinators detect confusion over CHPA, people coordinating the purchase at Dun & Bradstreet in Tampa seeing a great response from District 1.

As of July 1, 90 employees in 33 businesses will be covered through District 1's CHPA, said Marilynn Evert, assistant vice president.

A couple of weeks earlier, only two area businesses had signed up, Trocki said. Dun & Bradstreet has gotten more than 3 calls from District 1 since the telephone line opened May 16.

lliances will provide information on providers

Linda Zittler
's Journal

orida's new Community
lth Purchasing Alliances are
sed to provide consumers with
re than insurance.

he system soon will make avail-
e reports comparing perfor-
nces of insurance carriers and
lth care providers, said Debo-
A. Trocki, CHPA District 1
cutive director.

n initial function of CHPAs
: be to track customer satisfac-
1 with the insurance carriers
t offer plans to businesses with
and fewer employees.

· next spring, people consider-
CHPA will be able to browse a
sumer guide that summarizes
experiences of those who al-
iy joined.

"he quality companies wel-
te it because they're going to
e out on top and people are
ig to see why they should use
e businesses," Trocki said.
ie ones who need to improve
:r quality are going to be moti-
ed to do so or they are going to
: business."

tings on insurance carriers are
the start.

orida's CHPAs will link with
ting data bases, such as ones
that track hospital statistics and
disease reports A schedule span-
ning two years Lists reports for
release to consumers.

Most of the information will be
compiled through the state's
Agency for Health Care Administration, which is charged with providing an "information foundation" for health-care reform.

In the works are reports such as
the Consumer Guide to Hospital
Performance, to be released in November. The guide will compare
hospitals by resources and quality
of care. Direct comparisons include average length of stay, average gross charges, readmission
rates and mortality rates for medical and surgical patients.

Such comparisons are tricky,
medical officials said.

"If it is gathered accurately and
presented accurately, it can help
educate the public," said Dr.
Donna Jacobi, president of the
Escambia County Medical Society
and a partner at the Medical Center Clinic, who treats the elderly.

"But numbers can be misleading
if you don't have background. If
somebody looked at my mortality
rate it would be horrible, but you
have to realize the patients I see
are the ones most likely to die."

Hospitals officials are working
with AHCA to make comparisons
clearer and more fair.

"Clearly, we have a lot of concerns that whatever it is that they
elect to publish for the general
public is helpful instead of more
confusing," said Mike King, vice
president of financial planning
and analysis for Baptist Health
Care. "It's hard to compare one
hospital to another because the
patients are not the same."

For example, gross costs are
likely to be higher at Baptist H
pital than at others because
much cost is shifted to those '
can pay from Baptist's high 1
centage of patients who ex-
That population usually ha
wait longer for medical atten-
making their problems m
costly to treat, King said.

"If we put information out t
without the education that o.
to go along with it, we're at risl
people going to get their care '
places they really shouldn't."

HEALTH PLAN Q AND A

The following are common questions and their answers taken from the Health Plan Summary for the District 1 Community Health Purchasing Alliance.

Q. Who is eligible to join a CHPA?

A. Florida small businesses with 50 or fewer employees are eligible for health plan coverage. An eligible employee must work full time, defined as 25 or more hours a week. A business may be as small as one person and still be eligible.

Q. What plans are available?

A. There are basically two kinds of plans — indemnity, which comes in several forms, and a health maintenance organization or HMO.

Indemnity is a traditional insurance plan that pays specific dollar amounts to the insured person for specified services and procedures without guaranteeing complete coverage for the full cost.

HMOs require subscriber members, except in a medical emergency, to use the services of designated physicians, hospitals or other medical care providers CHPA offers variations of both.

Q. What is the health plan benefit package offered through CHPAs?

A. The CHPA health plans include coverage for hospital care and in a provider's office, preventive medical and reproductive care, care such as home health or hospice provided as a substitute for hospital care, durable medical equipment, chemotherapy/radiation, X-rays, lab and diagnostic work and mental health care. The standard plan covers prescription drugs, the basic plan does not.

Q. What about an insurance agent?

A. You will need an insurance agent to assist you and your employees in enrolling in the plans you select.

Q. Do I have to join?

A. No Membership in a CHPA is strictly voluntary, but only members can purchase health-care coverage through the CHPAs

Q. Who controls the CHPA?

A. Each CHPA is guided by a local 17-member board of directors comprising 11 business representatives, three consumers, and three government representatives who respond to needs of employer members

Q. What about coverage for pre-existing medical conditions?

A. Coverage offered to small groups is "guaranteed issue" — you or your dependents cannot be turned down or dropped because of medical history or current health status An employee or covered dependent may be subject to a pre-existing condition waiting period depending on whether the person had qualifying previous coverage

Q. How are group premiums determined?

A. The law says that small-group products may base rates only on age, sex, county of residence, number of family members and tobacco use This is known as modified community rating Medical conditions or number of claims are not factors.

Q. How much does the employer have to pay?

A. No business is required to join a CHPA or to provide health care coverage to employees Employers who choose to do so will be expected under most health plans to participate in paying the cost of employee coverage. That cost will usually be half of the lowest monthly "employee-only" plan rate available to employees of that business.

Q. How often will rates change?

A Once you are enrolled, your rate will not change for a year, although individual premium amounts may change because of "life" events such as marriage, divorce, birth and death.

Q. What happens to my coverage if I change jobs?

A. If the employee goes to work for another business that purchases small-group coverage, the new employee may choose one of the plans the employer selected There will be no new pre-existing waiting period if the employee already has met a pre-existing waiting period under the previous policy and applies for the new coverage within 30 days after the old coverage expires.

Q. Do all dependents have to be covered?

A. Coverage is available for:
- Employee only
- Employee and spouse
- Employee and dependent children
- Employee, spouse and dependent children.

It is important to decide who will be covered at enrollment.

Q. What if an employee just does not want health-care coverage?

A. A person who is eligible for coverage, has no other coverage and simply does not want coverage through CHPA can decline. If the employee does not enroll, then the employee's dependents cannot enroll either.

Q I have offices and employees in two other cities in Florida. Do I have to join two other CHPAs if I want to insure them?

A. No. The employer becomes a member in the CHPA district where the business is located If an employer has employees who live outside Florida, those employees also are eligible for coverage.

Q. Will I be able to keep my present doctor?

A. A number of different plans will be offered within the CHPA. If you choose an indemnity plan, you may select any physician If you use a managed care plan (PPO EPO or HMO), you must select a physician within that plan's network to provide health-care services. You may want to ask you doctor which plans he or she belongs to and also check the provider listings of the plans before you make a selection.

Q Will different type plans cost the same or will the premium be the same for all plans?

A Premiums vary by carrier as well as by the type of plan (standard or basic), plan arrangement, deductible selected and whether individual or family coverage You will receive summaries of each carrier's plan along with rate information specific to your business to help you make informed decisions on which plans to offer employees.

Q Can I change my health plan once I join the CHPA?

A Yes You will have an opportunity to change your health plans annually during an open enrollment period.

Insurance alliance: pain or gain?

CHPA aims to help small businesses afford health care, but some perplexed

By MARY CHRIS JAKLEVIC
News-Press staff writer

Like many small businesses, Skinny Snacks is battling to trim its health insurance costs. The maker of low-fat corn chips on Metro Parkway in Fort Myers contracted with an employee leasing company to reduce insurance costs for its eight workers. Even so, it pays $125 per employee per month. That adds times. $1 an hour in labor costs, figures president Diane Huth.

Huth was eager to get quotes from one of Florida's new Community Health Purchasing Alliances, CHPAs, which are trying to make insurance more affordable for small businesses.

The objective is to pool the buying power of companies with 50 or fewer employees and the self-employed to get discounts and ultimately help their employers obtain coverage for their workers. Florida has 2.5 million uninsured people, and 89 percent of them are in households where someone works.

The CHPAs also are supposed to reduce paperwork for business owners and make comparisons easier by offering uniform plans.

But after meeting with her agent, Huth had more questions than answers.

Some companies varied rates by age, others did not. Some were managed care plans with limited provider network, others offered no choice.

"What I found was, the rates are all over the board, from $50 to $350 a unit," said Huth, who plans to continue studying. "I don't know enough about the rules yet to make an intelligent decision."

Small business owners are scrambling to learn whether CHPAs announced "chippas," will save them money or enable them to buy insurance for the first time. Unlike a purchasing alliances in President Clinton's health proposal, Florida's CHPAs are voluntary.

Paperwork must be filled by insurers for the first buy wave of plans, which start July 1.

Whether widely. Some companies, however, rates through the CHPA, others are lower outside the CHPA.

"Best advice: shop around."

The Florida Agency for Health Care Administration maintains CHPAs will save averaging 20 percent, and as high as 40 percent.

"I think most business people are going to find CHPA is a better deal for them," spokesman Ed Towey said.

See CHPA / 2D

MARC BEAUDIN/News-Press

CHPA TALK: Diane Huth, left, president of Skinny Snacks, listens to Trish Bartenbach, president of Fort Myers Insurance and Financial Services, and Scott Robertson of the Umbrella Group of Florida explain the CHPA plan.

CHPAs — COMMUNITY HEALTH PURCHASING ALLIANCES

Timeline

April 1993:
Florida passes health reform, creating 11 voluntary, nonprofit alliances to pool the purchasing power of small businesses and self-employed people.

September 1993:
State officials appoint 17-member board to run the District 8 CHPA, which covers Collier, Charlotte, Lee, Glades, DeSoto, Hendry and Sarasota counties.

January 1994:
CHPA 8 receive bids from health care providers and insurance companies, and called accountable health partnerships (AHPs).

March 1994:
CHPA 8 hires Dun & Bradstreet to administer and market the health plans.

May 1994:
A few businesses sign up for policies that will start June 1.

June 1994:
Computerized rate system goes online, allowing widespread participation. Many policies are expected to take effect July 1.

The system

The small business owner:

■ Call 1-800-4MY-CHPA
The toll-free line is run by Dun & Bradstreet. Operators answer questions, provide referrals to insurance agents and send out health plan summaries, rate cards and CHPA applications.

OR

■ Go to an insurance agent
Insurance agent provides quotes and completes enrollment form for the CHPA and the insurance plans.

How it works. The small business:

● Pays $25 to join District 8 CHPA plus $6 per month per employee.
● Chooses a least two plans for employees — three if more than 30 workers. Plans are standardized for comparison.
● Receives bill from Dun & Bradstreet. Any claims go through the insurance agent.

SOURCE: D&B, CHPA, News-Press files

DAYMOND GASCON / News-Press

FT. MYERS NEWS-PRESS — 6/12/94

CHPA: Health plan targets costs of care

From Page 1D

Some agents aren't so sure "I don't think anyone just outright should assume because it comes from the CHPA it's a good deal." said David Springer, owner of Florida Agency Service, which distributes insurance products to agents.

In fact, consumers can reap the benefits of Florida's 1993 health reform legislation whether they join a CHPA or not. The law guarantees access to coverage for small groups.

Some key changes:

• Insurers can set rates using only the following criteria: age, sex, county of residence, family size and tobacco usage.

• People with pre-existing conditions cannot be denied coverage or made to pay more. However, they may have to wait 12 or 24 months for coverage if they were not insured during the previous year. People with pre-existing conditions no longer lose coverage when they change jobs.

• Workers in specific industries cannot be denied coverage or charged more. On-site construction workers, pest control workers and race car drivers used to be more expensive to insure. No longer.

These are important strides. Before January, Skinny Snacks couldn't get insurance for one worker with a back condition and for the premature child of another.

The company gave those workers the money that would have gone to their insurance. "We added $125 to payroll and they did what they could do, put it in the bank to cover their medical bills or tried to find a policy on their own," Huth said.

Under the new law, every worker is insured, and at a reasonable rate, Huth said.

Access is one part of the insurance problem CHPAs target another barrier: cost.

When patients are uninsured and can't pay, doctors and hospitals pass on the costs then insurance rates increase. With more insured people, the cost of care would be spread more evenly. The total cost should dip because more people could get preventative and early treatment.

Some agents predict CHPAs will most benefit groups of less than 10, which pay the highest rates because they are relatively risky and costly to administrate.

Agent Reina Schlager said the CHPA offers deals on low-cost, catastrophic-type coverage. She said some preferred provider organizations, or PPOs, in the CHPA are "extremely underpriced."

For example, Schlager said, a husband and wife in their early 40s found a preferred provider organization (PPO) with a $250 deductible for $226 a month. Their current plan costs the same but has a $2,500 deductible.

Business complaints

But some small businesses are not pleased with the limited coverage offered through the CHPA. "If they're looking for dental, supplemental medical, life insurance — which will pick up the price — right now you have to go outside the CHPA," Schlager said.

Rates could change in a year, after companies adjust prices according to their volume of business through CHPAs.

The District 8 CHPA, which covers Southwest Florida, reported 7,000 phone calls requesting information, but officials said there is no count of the policies sold.

It will take months or years to judge whether CHPAs are worthy of national emulation, or wasteful bureaucracy.

Some agents already credit CHPAs with slowing rate increases and educating consumers. Critics point out that each of the 11 CHPAs has two layers: a 17-member appointed board and a company to administrate the plans. Each receives $275,000 a year from the state.

Bob Whitlock, president of Southwest Florida Insurance Associates, calls CHPAs "a bureaucratic nightmare" subsidized by Florida taxpayers.

And Springer said the state is "trying to solve an insoluble problem," since small businesses can never achieve the economies of scale that large businesses have.

Towey said there's "no state bureaucracy in this" since boards are comprised of business people, consumers and state worker representatives. He said CHPAs are made to be self-sustaining in two years.

The District 8 CHPA predicts a slow start and rapid expansion. It will conduct a marketing campaign later this year and begin to rate health plans on quality.

Many small business owners contacted by the News-Press still hadn't heard of CHPAs but were eager to learn. One was Alberta Halyard, owner of Miss B's Salon of Beauty on Thomas Street. She spends a fourth of her monthly income — $206 — on insurance.

Years ago Halyard had no insurance, and a hospital refused to treat her for gallstones until she was declared eligible for Medicaid, the federal-state program for the poor.

Now 58 she doesn't want to go through the ordeal of being uninsured ever again.

"I have to cut back on grocery bill and everything else, but you have to have health insurance," she said

Coalition sells governor's version of Florida ...alth Security

Continued from page 4

enrollees over 150 percent of poverty who also can afford to make more substantial premium contributions.

According to materials from the AHCA packet, Florida Health Security can expect its largest group of enrollees from the 150 to 200 percent of poverty group. An April 13 letter from Chiles to Senate President Pat Thomas argues, "Eliminating part of the premium between 150 and 250 percent [who pay a greater share of the premium], will ease the state share of program expense from 29 to 35 percent" and cost the state $1.8 billion in matching federal funds over the next five years.

That's because for FHS enrollees over the 150 percent of poverty mark, federal and employee contributions both will be more significant than funding from the state. According to figures provided by the AHCA, on an average individual monthly HMO premium of $116 for a worker sitting between 150 and 200 percent of the poverty level, the employee/employer contribution will be $336 and the federal contribution $65 compared to a state subsidy of just $15. Between 200 and 250 percent of poverty, the state contribution drops to just one dollar while the employee/employee portion increases to $50 and the federal side remains constant at $65 per month. The state's parsimony is accomplished by FHS program rules requiring the employee/employee contribution to make up 85 percent of the state subsidy for any individual or family over 150 percent of the poverty level, according to AHCA documents.

Added the FAHMO's Duff, "From an underwriting point of view, the difference is that people at 250 percent of poverty have some level of care, are accustomed to seek out and use some level of medical care, and are probably in a better state of health. [FHS] needs both groups, the wealthy as well as the healthy to [diffuse risk] and make the program work."

Indeed, an official at an indemnity plan that really has higher in-CHPA than out-of-CHPA premiums noted that carriers inability to spread their risks over large and economically diverse CHPA enrollees already could drive up premium costs within the alliances. Since no employer premium contribution is required and individuals within small businesses still will make their own plan choice, low-bidding HMOs potentially

Continued on page 12

Health alliances to inch forward

Individuals and small businesses can start playing the group-insurance game Monday, but all the cards aren't on the table yet.

By Jeannie Kever
REGIONAL REPORTER

Florida's health-care reforms are supposed to become a reality on Monday, but the people in charge will forgive you if you're not first in line.

In fact, they might appreciate it.

"It's going to take us a while to get information out to people," said Sharon Rubright, an administrative assistant for the insurance-purchasing alliance whose jurisdiction includes Manatee County. "We don't want to have a massive enrollment right up front."

The alliance, officially known as the Region 6 Community Health Purchasing Alliance, is one of 11 organizations set up across the state to help small businesses buy health insurance.

Insurance companies have submitted bids to sell policies to members of the alliances. But comparison sheets allowing business owners to see what policies are available — and how much they will cost — aren't available yet.

Because of that, the alliance that covers Sarasota, Charlotte and DeSoto counties decided to put enrollment on hold.

"People will not remember that you were a week late, but they'll remember if the process does not go smoothly," said Alan Penn, the director of the Region 8 alliance. "I would rather be late and get it right."

He said he expects to begin enrollment about May 10.

The Region 6 alliance will begin contacting potential members and sending out enrollment forms on Monday, said Director Cynthia Sampson.

Each alliance, or CHPA (a term that bureaucrats pronounce "chippa"), will proceed at its own pace, said Ed Towey, a spokesman for the state Agency for Health Care Administration.

"On May 2, the CHPAs will be doing shakedown cruises, signing up people who have expressed interest, moving slowly so they can get the bugs out," he said.

Bids from insurance companies were opened in February, and the state has completed a major task certifying that the companies can deliver the promised services for the proposed rates. And Tom Foley,

an actuary with the state Department of Insurance, said premiums offered through the alliances will be about 10 percent below 1993 average market rates.

Monday is the state-set deadline for the alliances to begin operations, but there are no sanctions for alliances that take it more slowly. And nothing will kick into high gear at least until mid-May, when all of the comparison sheets should be ready.

Work on the sheets is underway. When they are ready for distribution to prospective members, the alliances expect to begin marketing in earnest.

Self-employed people and businesses with 50 or fewer employees will be able to buy the insurance. The actual purchase must be handled by an insurance agent, however.

And agents haven't seen the policies, either.

Penn plans two training sessions for insurance agents in Punta Gorda on May 10. Another training session will be held in Tampa on May 12, and

others are scheduled around the state.

The policies will be available only to alliance members.

The Region 6 alliance has set its annual membership fee at $25. Employers will also be charged $1 per month for each employee who signs up for health insurance, Rubright said.

Businesses with more than 50 employees can pay $100 a year to receive information about the various insurance plans, perhaps gaining leverage to renegotiate their own health-care coverage.

The Region 8 alliance also set a $25 annual fee for small businesses. Its monthly charge will be $3 per employee.

SARASOTA HERALD-TRIBUNE / SATURDAY, APRIL 30, 1994

For more information

■ Community Health Purchasing Alliance, District 6, serving Manatee, Hillsborough, Hardee, Highlands and Polk counties. 1-813-689-8646.

■ Community Health Purchasing Alliance, District 8, serving Sarasota, Charlotte, Collier, DeSoto, Glades, Hendry and Lee counties. 1-800-GET-CHPA or 1-813-630-6664.

Associate memberships for larger businesses in Region 8, which stretches from Sarasota County to Collier County, will be offered on a sliding scale: $100, $300 and $500. Businesses that pay more will be mentioned more often in the alliance newsletter.

Membership and enrollment fees are intended to help the alliances become self-sustaining. They will

receive $275,000 a year from the state for the first two years.

Monday's deadline for beginning enrollment is only the latest to be pushed back since the alliances were created under Florida's landmark health-care reforms approved in April 1993.

But Penn said the delay was predictable.

"There are just a lot of things to do," he said. "It's nobody's fault."

Officials in both Region 6 and Region 8 say they have heard from about 300 businesses interested in joining.

"We're so close, I can smell it," Penn said. "And it smells sweet."

CHPA seminar draws a crowd

By MICHELE CHANDLER
Herald Business Writer

A standing-room only crowd of more than 400 insurance agents; health-care firms and small business owners came to the first public seminar on the Community Health Purchasing Alliance of Dade and Monroe counties, seeking affordably-priced health insurance for small businesses.

State executives and alliance officials told the group that the novel brand of competition in Florida's health insurance industry that these new purchasing alliances would usher in would translate into lower insurance premiums.

Three out of every four insurance companies agreed to sell the same insurance plan more cheaply through the CHPA than on the open market, said Susan Pinnas, executive director of the Dade/Monroe CHPA. The average savings was 15 percent if bought through the CHPA, Pinnas said.

The alliances say they snared volume discounts on health-care costs by bringing together thousands of workers from small firms. By pooling their resources into a single, more powerful buyer, the CHPAs would command more bargaining clout with health insurance firms and negotiate lower rates. Monday is the first day insurance agents call sell the CHPA plans

Douglas Cook, director of the Florida Agency for Health Care Administration, said the competition spurred by the CHPAs has already contributed to lower health insurance premium costs since the beginning of the year.

PLEASE SEE CHPAS, 3C

CHPA seminar draws a crowd

CHPAS, FROM 1C

time one of these companies isn't getting any business?" said Tom Gallagher, commissioner of the Florida Department of Insurance." They're going to file a lower rate. They're going to have to figure out how to cut their costs.

According to state insurance department information Gallagher provided, a standard individual insurance plan with a $250 deductible sold by Centennial would cost $332.28 per month if sold through the CHPA, compared with a $378.18 for the same premium if sold independently. A Principal Mutual insurance plan — again with a $250 deductible — $289.04 inside the CHPA, compared with $309.63 if sold on the open insurance market.

Miami Herald 4/30/94

St. Pete

4B · TIMES ■ WEDNESDAY, MAY 18, 1994 · · · ·

Chiles kicks up his heels at kickoff

■ The governor celebrates the start of his health care reform and encourages small companies to pool together to buy health insurance.

By EDDIE DOMINGUEZ
Associated Press

Gov. Lawton Chiles dances the merengue with a Community Health Purchasing Alliance supporter Tuesday in Coral Gables.

MIAMI — With loud music and a little dancing Tuesday, Gov. Lawton Chiles launched a health insurance purchasing pool.

Encouraging small companies to buy their health insurance through a Community Health Purchasing Alliance, Chiles wore a train engineer's hat and called for everyone to jump on board the "CHPA Express."

Republicans helped pass a 1993 law forming 11 alliances throughout the state, but they've balked at the governor's latest proposal subsidizing private insurance for people who make up to $26,400, or 2½ times the poverty level.

Republicans charge Chiles would railroad the state into the largest entitlement program in Florida's history.

Ignoring criticism, Chiles was in town to have a good time and celebrate the implementation of his 1993 health care reform program. The insurance pools began offering coverage statewide May 2.

The state program created 11 districts in which employers can buy health insurance through the regional alliances. The idea is to pool small businesses so they can buy insurance at the same prices as large companies.

In a Clintonlike health care show, Chiles paraded people on stage as living examples of companies using the alliances to save money.

Fredric Hoffman said his 10-lawyer firm was faced with skyrocketing insurance costs. The firm's monthly bill went from $700 several years ago to more than $9,000.

"We had to eliminate raises and eliminate ... ," Hoffman said, adding that savings from the firm's participation in the alliance would provide relief. "For the first time, we're going to be able to offer our employees more choice for ss of a price."

Couple help pioneer Fla. alliances

Governor urges firms to join 'CHPA Express'

By GLENN SINGER
Staff Writer

Joyce and Kent Albu became pioneers this week in Florida's health care reform movement.

The young Delray Beach couple, who run a carpet design and installation business, were the first people in Palm Beach County to buy medical insurance through one of the state's 11 fledgling Community Health Purchasing Alliances, called CHPAs for short.

"I called a lot of companies, and the prices they wanted outside of the CHPA were outrageous We never could have afforded the rates," Joyce Albu said.

"Besides," she said, "the insurance companies wanted us to have at least $35,000 income to write a policy. My husband is just starting out. We didn't make that much money last year."

Inside the alliance, though, the couple has no minimum income requirement, and they will pay $186 38 a month for coverage through Blue Cross-Blue Shield's Health Options. That rate is one of the lowest among the companies that offer standard HMO coverage in Palm Beach County.

The goal of the alliances is to provide low-cost, quality health care to the estimated 2.7 million Floridians who are self-employed or work for firms that employ 50 or fewer employees

In Region 10. which covers Broward County. an estimated 40 000 small businesses employ 201.000 people. The Community Health Purchasing Alliance provides rates for 51 health plans offered by 34 companies

In Region 9. which covers Palm Beach County and four counties to the north and west. an estimated 37 290

PLEASE SEE CHPA / 8D

FROM PAGE 1D

Gov. Chiles urges businesses to use the new alliances

small businesses employ 205.000 people The purchasing alliance provides rates for 45 health plans offered by 36 companies.

In Palm Beach County, for example. insurance agents can offer 45 plans' health maintenance organizations. preferred provider organizations and indemnity coverage

Encouraging small companies to buy their health insurance through a purchasing alliance. Gov Lawton Chiles wore a train engineer's hat in Miami on Tuesday morning and called for everyone to jump on board the "CHPA Express." He later enrolled an alliance member in Titusville.

"We are now going to buy health care the way we buy every other product, for the best value at the lowest price." Chiles said. Some of the alliances started to enroll members as early as May 2.

Florida is one of several states experimenting with managed competition, the heart of President Clinton's proposal for national health care reform Republican leaders charge, however, that Chiles is railroading the state into the largest entitlement program in Florida's history.

Insurance agents are carefully watching evolution of the program studying the rates to see whether companies do offer better prices within the alliances.

"CHPAs definitely have a place for owners of small business who are just starting out." said insurance agent Gary Donahue of Delray Beach. who sold Joyce and Kent Albu their policy. "In time, if rates become more and more competitive, the idea could work for many more people"

For more information about the purchasing alliances. and to determine if a business or self-employed person qualifies for coverage, call 587-7108 in Broward County or 1-800-469-2472 in Palm Beach County

---

MAY 18 1994

FT. LAUD. SUN SENT

Alliance insures first members

By STEPHANIE L. JACKSON
Palm Beach Post Staff Writer

DELRAY BEACH — A self-employed man who has never had health insurance and hasn't seen a doctor in six years was enrolled Tuesday with his wife as the first members of the local Community Health Purchasing Alliance

Kent Albu, a 28-year-old carpet installer and rug-designer, and his wife, Joyce, 29, filled out papers last week so they could receive coverage in June.

"We're pretty relieved," Joyce Albu said. "We're both going to go in for checkups immediately, get our cholesterol checked and make sure we're healthy and sound."

The Delray Beach couple signed up for a standard benefits package under Health Options, the HMO offered by Blue Cross/Blue Snield. Coverage will cost $186 38 a month. Another HMO costs slightly less, but the Albus prefer the doctors and hospitals available through Health Options.

The alliance's offerings cost far less than earlier quotes of up to $500 on the outside. Joyce Albu said. "If we did not have the CHPA we could not afford insurance," she said

Her husband has been denied coverage because he had a one-man business or wasn't making enough money, she said They learned about the alliance from their insurance agent, Gary Donahue, who attended a CHPA training session last week

The alliance for Palm Beach County and the Treasure Coast is one of 11 established last year under state health-care reform to pool insurance buyers and lower costs. Businesses with one to 50 employees are eligible. Information is available by calling 1-800-4MY-CHPA during business hours

2C   Pensacola News Journal   Saturday, May 21, 1994

LOCAL

Steve Mawyer/News Journal

Gov. Lawton Chiles speaks Friday at a Pensacola business forum to help small businesses enroll in the Pensacola Area Community Health Purchasing Alliance.

Purchasing alliance gets first business

The first small business to buy insurance through the Pensacola-area purchasing alliance did so Friday.

James Lee and Associates, an insurance company, bought a plan for three employees and will pay $411 monthly instead of $709 monthly, according to Gov. Lawton Chiles' press office.

Chiles was among those on hand Friday at a business forum in Pensacola to help tell small businesses how to enroll in the Pensacola Area Community Health Purchasing Alliance, one of 11 statewide.

The alliances pool the purchasing power of self-employed individuals and small businesses.

The health alliances were formed as part of health care reform Chiles supported last year.

During the gathering Friday, Chiles also pushed for passage of the Florida Health Security program.

That program would use funds from Medicaid savings to pay private insurance for more than 1 million people who have no insurance.

Chiles may call the Legislature back to the Capitol the week of June 6 for a special session on the proposal.

Health care reform is the major unresolved issue from the regular session that ended in April.

The House passed a plan but the Senate refused to tackle the issue in the waning days of the session.

MAY 29 1994

FLA. TIMES UNION

Chippa: Cure or confusion?

By Chuck Springston
Business writer

The letters CHPA officially stand for "community health purchasing alliance," a new state program intended to provide low-cost medical insurance to small businesses.

But for many businesses, they might just as well stand for "confusing health plan alternative."

Even though the alliances — commonly called "chippas" — were created by legislation more than a year ago, they're still not something the average person at a cocktail party could lead a discourse on for very long.

Yet just about everyone knows health care reform is a big deal on the political agenda. And chippas — easily understood or not — are at the center of Florida's reform effort.

That's going to become even more apparent over the next several weeks. This is the first month businesses can join chippas to get health care insurance.

And chippa administrators will be stepping up their advertising and marketing campaigns in the coming months. The chippas no longer will be just an untested political theory.

"It's time that this whole discussion of the chippa move out of the political arena into the nuts-and-bolts arena of how it can be made effective," said Edgar

Schneider

M. Dunn Jr., chairman of Northeast Florida's chippa.

As that happens, just about any Florida business, big or small, that offers health insurance to its employees — or would like to — will need a basic understanding of what chippas are and how they work.

What follows is a guide to help get you started.

In the beginning . . .

Gov. Lawton Chiles and the Florida Legislature created the chippas during the 1993 session. Chiles signed the bill into law April 29 of last year.

The law, in short, creates a new system for buying and selling health insurance — a voluntary system that relies on the forces of private enterprise but also sets up new government-chartered organizations as intermediaries between the buyers and sellers.

Those intermediaries are the chippas.

Chippas provide a way for a region's small businesses to join an alliance that gives them some of the same advantages big companies get when buying health insurance.

For chippa purposes, a small business is a company with 50 or fewer workers, including self-employed people and sole proprietors.

There are 11 chippas across the state, each covering one to 16 counties. The Northeast Florida chippa comprises seven counties and is based in Daytona Beach.

Each chippa is governed by a 17-member board, appointed by the governor, Senate president and House speaker.

The chippa's meetings and records are public, although the financial and medical information collected from businesses remains confidential, said Ed Towery, a spokesman for the Agency for Health Care Administration. "It's not open to public scrutiny."

All the board appointments were completed by Oct. 1, putting a key component of the buying side of the reform equation into place.

On the selling side is another new organization, called an "accountable health partnership," or AHP.

An AHP is, at its core, an insurance company, although many are part of networks that also include hospitals, doctors, pharmacies and other health care providers. Only state-certified AHPs can sell policies to chippa members.

The chippa itself doesn't buy health plans from AHPs.

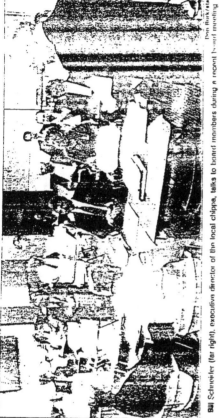

Bill Schneider (far right), executive director of the local chippa, talks to board members during a recent board meeting

Don Burk/staff

Instead, the chippa asks AHPs to submit proposals based on specifications from the board, then puts together information that helps businesses compare the proposals.

Businesses get to pick the plans they want for their employees.

The local chippa made its request for AHP proposals Dec. 17. The proposals were turned in Feb. 10.

Much of the chippa's administrative work, as well as marketing and advertising help, is being handled by Tampa-based Dun & Bradstreet Plan Services Inc., which signed a contract April 22 to be a "third-party administrator."

The chippa's own staff consists only of Executive Director Bill Schneider and a secretarial position. However, the Tallahassee staff of the Agency for Health Care Administration also helps out.

Last week, Dun & Bradstreet hooked up a toll-free number — (800) 469-2472 for businesses that want information on

"The minute it was figured on, our phones started ringing," said Marilynn Evert, assistant vice president of marketing for Dun & Bradstreet Plan Services.

The chippa hopes to have some of these rallies through the process and receiving coverage June 1.

Down to business

The chippa concept is supposed to wipe away at least some of the disadvantages small businesses have faced buying insurance.

Small businesses traditionally pay higher premiums than big businesses because insurers consider them riskier customers. If one employee in a 10-person company develops a serious illness, there aren't as many co-workers paying premiums to cover those costs as there are in a 100-person company.

The chippas themselves don't offer much help there. After all, each business in the chippa still is buying insurance

separately, not collectively as one large pool.

But the 1993 law requires insurers selling policies to small businesses — in or out of the chippa — to use something called "modified community rating."

Essentially that means insurers must blend all the small companies they cover into a geographic area — a whole county — before figuring the premiums.

In "pure" community rating, everybody in the county pays the same rate. Florida's modified community rating for small businesses allows insurers to adjust rates within a county to account for differences in age, sex, tobacco use and family size.

Risks and ratings aside, the chippa may be a bigger help in the other areas where small businesses are at a disadvantage.

Small businesses frequently pay more because there are more of a hassle for insurers administratively to account for

Regional chippa

rate for 500 people if they're all in one big company rather than spread out over dozens of small companies.

The chippa will take on some administrative tasks normally performed by insurance companies, such as determining eligibility for coverage and collecting premiums. Insurers should be able to pass on those savings as lower rates.

Finally, big companies often have the advantage of big employee-benefits departments with the time and staff to research dozens of health plans for the best deal.

The chippa will perform that job for its small businesses.

The premiums

It's difficult to generalize on the savings possible through the chippa because every business has a different mix of ages, gender, family size and smoking habits.

But the chippa did ask AHPs, when they returned their proposals in February, to calculate the premiums for two sample companies.

Based on those examples, the discounts inside the chippa, compared with identical plans sold outside the alliance, ranged from less than 1 percent to about 12 percent, with most less than 5 percent.

AvMed Health Plan, which offers about 5 percent average price break inside the chippa, doesn't want to offer deeper discounts until it gets a better feel for that impact the alliance will have, said Pat Nelson, executive director for the North Florida region.

Some AHPs didn't offer any discounts to chippa members. Among them: Jacksonville-based Blue Cross and Blue Shield of Florida.

Blue Cross is offering about the same rates inside and outside the chippa because the benefits package and target market are the same, said Craig Thomas, director of state business.

"We have no experience with the chippa yet," Thomas said. "As we get experience — not just medical experience but administrative experience — the rates may in fact end up different than our out-of-chippa rates.

Dunn, the chippa chairman, said: "I believe the first bids that came out of the chippa are not our best shot. That's the first time we've loaded and fired and we haven't started firing for effect yet."

The chippa's ultimate ambition is to develop health-plan comparisons that go far beyond price.

It wants to compile information on how the AHPs stack up in quality of care. Does one AHP have a better survival rate for heart patients? Or more success in detecting breast cancer early?

Also, the chippa will report the results of customer-satisfaction surveys AHPs are required to conduct.

Chippa theorists hope all of this intense, public scrutiny will encourage health care companies to improve quality and cut costs.

"It's either going to make or break the marketing efforts of some of these companies," Dunn said.

Big companies, as well as small ones, will be able to tap into the chippa's files on AHPs.

Although companies with more than 50 workers can't buy insurance through the chippa, they can still become "associate members," entitling them to the quality and price data collected by the alliance.

"That will give their health benefits manager the ability to track this on an ongoing basis," said Schneider, the chippa executive director.

The plans

For businesses that do buy insurance through the chippa, there's not much variety in the level of coverage among the various plans.

All AHPs are required by the chippa to offer two benefits packages developed by the state Department of Insurance.

The department calls them "basic" and "standard" benefits packages. In general, the standard package covers more services and pays more of the medical bill.

Although limiting coverage options, the requirement that all AHPs offer the same two benefit packages enables employers to make apples-to-apples price comparisons

---

IN CHARGE OF THE CHIPPA

Each of the state's community health purchasing alliances, or "chippas," is run by a 17-member board of directors. The governor appoints nine members. The president of the state Senate and the speaker of the House each appoint four. Board members serve a three-year term and are not paid for their service. Here are the 17 people who make up the chippa board for Region 4, which covers Northeast Florida.

Chairman Edgar M. Dunn Jr., attorney, owner of Dunn Hardware, Daytona Beach.

Vice Chairman Charles H. Liphart, owner, Charles Liphart & Son Jacksonville.

Secretary Linda P. Major, community relations, Daytona International Speedway, Daytona Beach.

Treasurer Jack A. Collier, account executive, Dean Witter Reynolds Inc., Jacksonville.

T. Wayne Bailey, political science professor, Stetson University, Deland

Talmadge L. Bennett, vice president, Bill Williams Air Conditioning & Heating Inc., Jacksonville

Herbert C. Brattlof, president, H. Brattlof Construction Co. Inc., Palm Coast

Douglas Brown, loan specialist, First Coast Black Business Investment Corp., Jacksonville

Queen E. Cherry, city councilwoman, Lake Helen

Otis A. Mason, former superintendent of schools, St. Johns County, St. Augustine

W. Guy Odum Jr., owner, Odum Properties, Ponte Vedra Beach

Anita M. Rink, management consultant, Flagler Beach

Diana J. Rio, benefits manager, IT&T, Ormond Beach

Thomas F. Slater, attorney, Jacksonville

Janie Q. Thomas, owner, Thomas Live Shrimp, Fernandine Beach

Donna P. Williams, human resources director, The Florida Times-Union, Jacksonville

Katharine E. Wilson, chief quality and compliance officer, CSX Transportation Inc., Jacksonville.

Additionally the AHPs still can offer a ters of plans to provide that coverage ough traditional health insurance or ough programs such as health .ntenance organizations and preferred .ider organizations which give counts when patients go to specified tors and hospitals

In Northeast Florida, about 30 AHPs .ve signed one year agreements. ectiv. May 1 to offer plans in the .gion. These AHPs sell different plans Each business that joins the chippa is .quired to give employees a choice of at .ist two plans and businesses with more

.an 4 workers must offer at least three.

chippa rules say AHPs must offer .ans that require employers to pay a .rcent of the workers' premium equal to .i percent of the lowest-cost plan the .mployer offers.

For example if a small business offers . HMO that costs $100 a month in .remiums and a traditional plan that .osts $160 the employer's share is $50 in .oth cases.

Some plans may be available for .mployer contributions less than 50 .ercent but likely will cost more.

Insurers generally want employers to .ay part of the premium because it .ncourages more employees to sign up .nd spreads the risk.

Otherwise some employees might not .e able to afford coverage. And those .eople who opt out will most likely be .he healthiest workers, leaving the sickest .n the pool

The premium includes a built-in .ervice charge of $4 per employee per .onth — $3 to Dun & Bradstreet and $1 .o the chippa for operational expenses.

There are no other membership fees .r businesses that buy coverage through .e chippa. But big companies and others .hat join only for the information services .ay a $20 per month fee.

The day will come, Schneider .redicted, when big businesses may wish .ey could take advantage of the chippa's .ther features as well.

"I think the time will rapidly approach .here our small businesses are actually .oing to be getting better rates and better .rvice than some of the large groups." .e said.

5 steps to health coverage

Here are the steps an employer typically will take to participate in Florida's new community health purchasing alliances, or chippas designed to provide low-cost health coverage to smaller companies.

STEP 1

Employer calls toll-free number (800 4my chpa) to request application for chippa membership and insurance. Call answered by chippa's administrative agent, Dun & Bradstreet Plan Services, which mails out application, booklet describing available health plans, rate sheets comparing prices and enrollment material.

STEP 2

Employer sits down with his or her insurance agent to review health plans and costs. Agent calculates what the premiums would be. Dun & Bradstreet is developing a computer system to enable the agent to call and get a fast premium calculation. D&B eventually will provide agents with diskettes that let them do essentially the same thing on their own computers.

STEP 3

Employer picks insurance plans it will offer employees. Employer writes check for first month's premium (or uses electronic funds tranfer). Even if a business buys three separate plans from three different insurers, it writes just one check. Agent sends check, chippa application, other forms to D&B.

STEP 4

D&B verifies information on forms, making sure employer meets criteria for chippa membership (such as no more than 50 employees). D&B deposits check in chippa's account. Money then dispensed to appropriate insurers.

STEP 5

D&B forwards enrollment information to insurer, which mails out policyholder booklets and ID cards. Coverage generally begins on first day of the following month.

— Steve Nelson/staff

Mr. TOWNS. Mr. Adkins.

Mr. ADKINS. Mr. Chairman, members of the committee, thank you for inviting me here to share with the subcommittee consumer perspectives on the issues of voluntary health care alliances as well as to offer suggestions about what kind of Federal guidance may be necessary to provide to the States.

My name is Jason Adkins. I am executive director of the Center for Insurance Research based in Boston, which is a public policy research and advocacy institute. We have been involved in the health care process primarily through NAIC's—National Association of Insurance Commissioners—deliberations where we have been working for a number of years. The NAIC is made up of the state insurance regulators, as you know, and they are now in the process of developing four model guidelines/laws for States in terms of the structures of alliances as well as developing eight model standards on all aspects of quality delivery of health care.

And we have been very involved in that process and have written extensively about what kinds of protections are necessary for consumers. At any point this committee is interested we would be happy to share that material with you.

The legislative process of which we are now involved was, of course, inspired by the need to provide coverage, health care coverage to the 38 million people in this country who are currently uninsured, as well as to protect those millions of people who risk losing their coverage due to change of jobs and other circumstances.

We are heartened that Congress is considering guarantee issue protections as well as eliminating pre-exclusions. But we feel that health care reform needs to move beyond limited market reforms to strong mandatory standards to protect consumers. Neither of the above reforms I just mentioned give access to standard package of benefits that are fairly priced and offer an adequate choice of competent and high quality providers on their own.

States must be given the option to establish a variety of health care reforms including a single-payer system or health care purchasing alliances which will provide those kinds of benefits.

I reserve my comments now to the issue of the alliances. I was asked by you and your staff to speak briefly to the benefits and problems of alliances from the consumer perspective. The benefits seem clear. GAO has outlined them. We agree with most of their findings.

Alliances help spread the risk to a large pool. They allow sharing of administrative costs and create economies of scale, which is where we think a lot of the savings come from.

We have concerns about cost shifting, which GAO should also look into in terms of the lower loss ratio cost. And we see that alliances can become powerful market forces in the marketplace which can drive down prices through their negotiating capacity. We support the idea that alliances should be able to negotiate with health plans on behalf of their members.

At this date much attention has already been given to the unaccountable and bureaucratic problems of alliances. We won't go into that now, but I would like to share our concerns about what alliances might look like in the future by looking at what the NAIC has just promulgated in terms of its first model guideline for alliances.

They have established a fairly government heavy bureaucracy which puts what is called a State Board in the Department of Insurance in the State. That State board negotiates with the health plans for coverages. It establishes the minimum benefits. It also integrates with the alliances, which are effectively administrative entities for the small employers who are eligible.

But an alliance those—that board of directors, which is elected by the employers, none of the employees, can be removed by the State Board, the State agency arm, and the State Board approves the funding, the principal funding mechanism for the alliances. So, we have seen them create a network of fairly involved government intervention in the health care structure, which concerns us.

In terms of accountability of the Boards, the State Board has up to nine members, only two of whom are employees. The others are representing other interests outside of the ultimate end-user whom we are most concerned about. There is some effort to provide for diversity of representation which we are pleased to see.

The alliances have no representation for the end-user, that is, the employees. Simply stated, this structure is unaccountable to consumers, too State dominated and too bureaucratic.

In terms of Federal guidance to the State, minimum Federal standards are appropriate to ensure the alliances are sufficiently accountable to consumers and designed to provide large numbers of people with access to high quality health care delivered in a cost efficient manner. The NAIC models, no matter their caliber, would not be sufficient to meet—to establish those minimum standards because NAIC models are voluntary to the States.

There are a number of structural and procedural protections we believe are essential to ensure that alliances can perform effectively and to the benefit of consumers. Alliances should be structured so that there is maximum access, that means to facilities, quality providers, a range of coverages, and grievance procedures and internal mechanisms for dispute resolution.

Consumers must also be protected from loss of coverage or benefits due to the actions of others, such as employers. If employers terminate coverage, fail to continue to qualify for coverage or otherwise place coverage in jeopardy, consumers must have continuation protection.

Meaningful choice. Consumers must have a full range of choices and options to choose in their health plans. This does not mean, however, that they need to be overwhelmed with the full gamut of health plan options in the marketplace. They need meaningful choices in the health plan through prudent purchasing power, that is the power to negotiate with the health plans, and should be able to limit the number of plans offered. But again, caveats are that maximum access to a variety of coverage is available.

Geographic area is another critical question. Florida, fortunately, uses the SMSA as its essential central point for defining its alliance territory. We are concerned that without an SMSA limitation on alliances, and also on rating territories, that geographic area will be used as a surrogate for income and ethnicity by alliances and health plans, particularly if they are permitted to subdivide urban areas. The alliance model developed by the NAIC, the first one I have mentioned, currently allows a 3-digit differential which, according to a quick analysis we did of Chicago—and we intend to look at other cities—shows that that will allow for surrogacy for ethnicity and income.

Of course, governance, which is the main issue you have asked me to speak to, is a critical one. The politicization problem discussed by GAO is a serious one, although we applaud the Florida effort to include diversified groups representing the community served by the alliances.

Voting is another possibility, and where directors are elected or appointed, we believe that strong criteria is important to minimize interested parties from the provider end or others to be involved. And I should point out that where there are elections we are also concerned that large employers or particularly well-organized industry or trade associations could dominate an alliance board candidate election process.

Mr. TOWNS. Mr. Adkins, if you could summarize. Your 5 minutes has expired.

Mr. ADKINS. Let me summarize by saying that we believe another critical point is that citizens be involved in the process, not only in terms of the composition of the boards of the alliances or any State agency regulating it, but that there also be another independent entity through which they can organize themselves and participate actively in dealing with issues related to the alliance as well as the health care system generally.

We have submitted a proposal to you which is now being considered by the NAIC for the creation through State authority of a Consumer Health Insurance Board that allows consumers to establish their own organization which is democratically controlled. Consumers find each other through access to the billing enclosures of alliances or health plans, and they are in that way able to fund themselves as well as to participate actively in the process and to represent consumer interests. We think that these organizations that will be important as well as this body in helping to develop quality care standards, procedures and practice guidelines which are essential for protecting consumers.

Thank you.

Mr. TOWNS. Thank you very much.

[The prepared statement of Mr. Adkins follows:]

TESTIMONY OF

JASON B. ADKINS

EXECUTIVE DIRECTOR,
CENTER FOR INSURANCE RESEARCH
BEFORE THE
SUBCOMMITTEE ON
HUMAN RESOURCES AND INTERGOVERNMENTAL RELATIONS
JUNE 30, 1994

Mr. Chairman, members of the Committee, thank you for inviting me to share with this subcommittee consumer perspectives on the issue of voluntary health care purchasing alliances and to offer suggestions concerning how the federal government can provide guidance to the states that will ensure consumers are adequately protected. My name is Jason Adkins and I am executive director and an attorney with the independent, nonprofit Center for Insurance Research (Center) which is based in Boston, Massachusetts. The Center is a research, public policy and advocacy organization which has focused on health care reform from the consumer perspective principally at the national level through active participation in the deliberations of the National Association of Insurance Commissioners (NAIC). The NAIC is composed of all the state insurance regulators and is currently developing model laws and regulations governing health care alliances and a broad array of medical quality assurance and related standards.

The legislative process of which I am now apart was inspired by the need to address the critical problem of the uninsured, who number 38 million people in the United States today, and the millions of others who risk losing their health insurance coverage. I am heartened that Congress is poised to adopt guarantee issue requirements and prohibit pre-existing condition exclusions, but health care reform needs to move beyond such simple market reforms to strong mandatory minimum standards to protect consumers. Neither of the above reforms will give consumers access to a standard package of benefits that are fairly priced and offer an adequate choice of competent, high quality providers. Market reforms alone are not enough. States must be given the option to establish a variety of health care reforms, including a single-payer system or health care purchasing alliances that will provide a minimum package of fairly priced benefits with adequate consumer protections. My comments here are reserved to voluntary alliances given the focus of this subcommittee.

BENEFITS OF AND PROBLEMS WITH ALLIANCES

The benefits of alliances to participating consumers are that they spread the risk of medical costs over a large pool, allow sharing of administrative costs and become powerful market forces capable of negotiating lower premiums and better coverages with health plans competing for their business. Many existing public and private alliances bear these principles out. Where there are adequate structural and consumer protections, alliances should achieve many of the goals of increasing access and lowering the costs of health care. They do not, however, achieve universal coverage in the voluntary market context on their own.

At this late date, attention has already focused on alliances as potentially unaccountable and too bureaucratic. The General Accounting Office (GAO) report discussed here today provides some insights into those matters. Our concerns about alliances are perhaps best described in the context of the NAIC model purchasing alliance guidelines which were exposed for public comment this month. The model NAIC statute establishes a government-heavy bureaucracy, creating a State Board within the department of insurance that has effective control over a number of noncompeting regional alliances which exist as mere administrative bodies for small employers. In effect, the alliances are extensions of the state agency which has ultimate authority to remove the alliance board and approve the alliances' principle source of funding (employer surcharges). The State Board, not the alliances, negotiates with health plans and establishes the standard benefit plans. The State Board is controlled by up to nine appointees, only two of whom are employees. There is no organized consumer representative. The alliance boards are even less accountable. Although the member employers elect the alliance board of directors, there is no provision for employees to vote or serve on the board.
Simply stated, this structure is unaccountable to consumers, too state dominated and too bureaucratic.

FEDERAL GUIDANCE TO STATES

Minimum federal standards are appropriate to ensure that alliances are sufficiently accountable to consumers and designed to provide large numbers of people with access to high quality health care delivered in a cost efficient manner. The NAIC model health care laws and guidelines, regardless of their caliber, will fail to guarantee consumers minimum essential protections because NAIC models are only voluntarily adopted by the states. Although we had a very limited time in preparing these remarks, what follows is a partial discussion of structural, procedural and quality assurance protections necessary under alliances.

Structural and Procedural Protections

Accessibility

Alliances should be structured so that small employers, employees and possibly individuals have ready access to quality services and health benefits. Through the alliances, consumers must have access to an adequate, accessible, qualified network of providers, access to a reasonable range of benefits in a reasonable period of time, and access to fair and equitable grievance procedures, dispute resolution, remedies and comprehensive regulation.

Consumers must also be protected from loss of coverage or benefits due to the actions of others such as regulator, employers, health plans or alliances. If employers terminate coverage, fail to continue to qualify for coverage or otherwise place coverage in jeopardy consumers must have continuation protection.

Meaningful Choice

Consumer must have a full range of services and options from which to choose in their health plans. However, this does not mean they must be overwhelmed with a multitude of essentially indistinguishable choices. While all health plans available within a particular alliance would be available to the consumers in the alliance, consumer choices could be somewhat limited to the extent alliances have the authority to bargain on behalf of their members. We are concerned, however, that limitations of health plans could reduce the availability of experimental and innovative procedures and coverages. Protections must be established to ensure that such options continue to be available.

Geographic Area

Alliance territories should be as large as possible to ensure a broad spread of risk and should be no smaller than a Standard Metropolitan Statistical Area (SMSA). We are concerned that geographic area will be used as a surrogate for income and ethnicity by alliances and health plans, particularly if they are permitted to subdivide urban areas. A preliminary examination of demographics in the Chicago area which I conducted revealed the close relationship between income and three digit zip code areas. The resulting outcome would not be an improvement over our current system. Unfortunately, the NAIC has settled on the minimum three digit zip areas for rating purposes without adequate consideration of the ramifications of allowing divisions based on such relatively small geographic areas. This should not be permitted.

Governance

Consumers and employers must have equal representation and combined control a majority representation on all alliance boards and any agency oversight boards. Consumers must be represented on all advisory committees. It is not enough that employers are represented on the boards. Employees who receive the benefits must have an equal voice. The GAO discussion of the politicization of the appointment process in Florida suggests that greater oversight is necessary, and that elections may be a more appropriate means of selecting the board. Whether directors are elected or appointed, strict eligibility criteria should be adopted to ensure balanced consumer representation and participation and preclude providers, health plans and other such interested parties from participating on the boards. It should be made explicit that no licensee of the Department of Insurance, an agent of a licensee, or a party receiving compensation from a licensee or agent of a licensee, or the immediate family member of any such person, will be eligible to be an alliance board member. Neither should a person who is employed by, affiliated with an agent of, or otherwise a representative of any carrier or health care provider, or the immediate family member of any such person be eligible for the alliance boards.

Where there are elections, we are also concerned that larger employers, or particularly well-organized industries or trade associations could dominate an alliance board candidate election process. This lends support to the proposition that alliance boards be composed of both employers and employees in equal number (individuals should also be included in equal number if individuals are included in the alliances). To the extent possible, measures to limit the power of such organized entities over the election process should be considered.

Procedural Accountability
Alliance boards should be subject to an open meeting provision to ensure adequate opportunity for consumer participation and access to information. We believe that public meetings provide a strong incentive for employee and other representatives on the boards to remain accountable to their constituents.

Authority to Negotiate
We support the principle that alliances have the authority to conduct prudent purchasing with health plans to facilitate meaningful competition. Without the authority to bargain on behalf of consumers, the alliances will become mere administrative conduits and therein will fail to realize their potential as bargaining agents for consumers. The findings in the GAO report demonstrates that this function is important to existing alliances for lowering premiums.

Funding
Funding may be derived from surcharges on employers or by other permissible means, but explicit restrictions should be established. No funds should be permitted to be received through grants, surcharges or appropriation from any private individual or entity that is in any way affiliated with a licensee of the Department of Insurance, an agent of a licensee, or a party receiving compensation from a licensee or agent of a licensee, and no one employed by, affiliated with an agent of, or otherwise a representative of any carrier, health plan, provider, health care professional or association. This is important to ensure that board members are not financially influenced by industry representatives, and to promote public confidence in the alliances.

Conflicts of Interest

In addition to the limiting potential financial conflicts discussed above, it is important to limit potential conflicts of interest in decision making. This could be accomplished through the enactment of a six month post-employment restriction on alliance board members and officers, and a one year post-employment restriction on the executive directors of the boards. Such a provision is also necessary to bolster public confidence in the process.

Ombudsman

An ombudsman must be established to assist consumers with their questions and concerns about alliances and health care system more generally. The ombudsman should be outside the alliances themselves to avoid the predictable limitations such a close institutional nexus would create. A program modeled after the State Long-Term Care Ombudsman Program mandated by the Older Americans Act that serves consumers in nursing homes is one meritorious model. We recommend that the subcommittee also consider another model which is revenue neutral for taxpayers. The Consumers Health Insurance Board, or CHIB, is a self-funded, democratically-controlled, consumer membership organization that could address consumer complaints within the alliances, but could also represent consumers as a class in the health care system. Attached is a more detailed description of the CHIB and model state legislation which the NAIC State and Federal Health Insurance Legislative Policy Task Force has agreed to consider. Federal authorization for such an organization would also be appropriate.

Quality Assurance

Quality of care and quality outcome measures and practice guidelines must not be left to the alliances or health plans to develop and enforce. The managed care industry has been in this position which has resulted in serious complaints from consumers who cannot always get care when it is required. The Medicare Risk program is a good example of the kinds of problems consumers experience in a very restricted managed care environment. A 1993 study by the Center for Health Care Rights in Los Angeles found that "Medicare enrollees received 50 percent less home health visits than Medicare fee-for-service beneficiaries" and that "HMO referral and utilization control systems were used to delay and to deny needed care." *Medicare Advocate* (Spring 1993).

The most critical aspects of health care delivery must not be left to the alliances themselves to define. Federal standards for medical quality assurance, utilization review, provider credentialing and contracting, data reporting, confidentiality and grievance procedures, among other areas, are essential to protect consumers and appropriate in the context of alliances. Special provisions should be made to apply them appropriately.

It is critical that full information is available to health plans, alliances, regulators and public about health plan diagnoses, treatments, utilization rates, outcomes, costs of care, complaints, among other indications of quality. Alliances must be involved in monitoring health plan quality and making summary reports available to consumers.

We have provided extensive comments on all these matters to the NAIC and will make these materials available to this subcommittee upon your request.

CONCLUSION

States should have the option to establish health care purchasing alliances as a mechanism for increasing consumer access to high quality health care delivered in a cost effective manner. Federal standards are necessary to ensure that alliances do not become unaccountable or over bureaucratic.

Thank you for the opportunity to present our views to this subcommittee. I am prepared to take your questions.

CENTER FOR INSURANCE RESEARCH
11 Stillings Street, 2nd Floor, Boston, MA 02210

CONSUMER HEALTH INSURANCE BOARDS: AN ESSENTIAL COMPONENT OF STATE HEALTH CARE REFORM

Health care insurance and delivery systems in the United States are currently undergoing massive reform at the state and federal level. One of the central purposes of all health care reform is to extend the services of health care services in a cost effective manner to the many Americans who have been unable to obtain health insurance. But even universal coverage would not, in and of itself, solve all the problems with health care in this country. Consumers need to be assured of access to high quality, equitably priced health care in a system that is fair, efficient and accountable to consumers and includes meaningful procedural and substantive protections. A self-funded, democratically-controlled, nonprofit, consumer membership organization is needed to accomplish these objectives. Below is a discussion of the rationale and precedent for such a Consumer Health Insurance Board (CHIB), as well as a brief description of the CHIB and how it would function. A model state statute to authorize such an organization is attached.

CONSUMER PROTECTION

How can consumers' interests be advanced in the complex and changing health care system? The Departments of Insurance and Attorneys General attempt to protect the consumer interest, but they tend to be overburdened and understaffed. Studies show that on average, less than six percent of the annual insurance premium taxes collected by states is spent on insurance regulation, and regulators lack the personnel and tools to fulfill their mission of providing adequate consumer protection in the area of insurer solvency, let alone market conduct. For example, the U.S. General Accounting Office (GAO) reported that 14 states did not have an actuary either on staff or under contract to work on health insurance. The GAO also found wide variations in the practices and procedures used to monitor insurer solvency, approve health insurance premium rates and policy forms, and respond to consumer complaints. Such variations led the GAO to note that questions have been raised about the states' capacity to adequately regulate the health insurance industry. As most of the proposed health care reform initiatives would require more state involvement in regulation and enforcement, the questions concerning their capacity to regulate become even more troublesome.

It is essential that strong protections for consumers are incorporated into the reform legislation. The current National Association of Insurance Commissioners (NAIC) draft alliance and health care accountability standards contain some important protections. However, the consumer protections in the NAIC standards are generally inadequate to the extent that they are embodied in a structure that relies almost exclusively on the government or employers for monitoring and enforcement. These purchasing alliance models are structured to be accountable to their boards of directors, but are fundamentally flawed because the models do not require that individual consumers be represented on those boards at all, let alone require a consumer majority. These alliances will be dominated by employers who will represent their interests with insurers, as is the case under the current failed system. Therefore, consumers will be protected only where the interests of employers and their employees intersect, and where regulatory agencies step in. But, even the state boards, which have primary jurisdiction over the alliances in the NAIC models, are similarly flawed having only two consumer seats (with Gubernatorial prerogative to appoint a third) out of a nine member board. This disassociated, regulatory-heavy approach is no different than the current system which inadequately represents consumers.

Consumers representatives must have significant representation on all alliance boards and any agency oversight boards. Even such representation would not be enough to adequately protect the interests of consumers, however, because the structure of the alliance boards would blunt the effectiveness of consumer participation. Purchasing alliances must represent several interests: state government, employers and consumers. As such, consumer interests compete with many interests. There may also be issues affecting consumers which are beyond the scope of the alliances or state boards. And as in any quasi-governmental entity, financial and political constraints may limit the capacity of the organization to address consumer concerns.

Consumer representation on the boards does not address another fundamental issue: all interested parties in the health care process are organized but consumers. Employers, insurers, doctors, hospitals and agents have their own powerful, well-funded national and state associations. Only consumers lack the organization, funding and technical assistance necessary to participate fully.

Previous attempts to mandate consumer representation on the boards of health organizations can inform this discussion. The Health Systems Agency (HSA) network of planning bodies, established under the National Health Planning and Resources Development Act of 1974, provides a telling example of boards which required a majority of consumer members but proved not to be a powerful source of protection for consumers. Health care providers and insurers were coordinated and well funded and thus were able to hire experts who were technically proficient and had the time and resources to devote to the HSAs. Consumers on the boards were generally volunteers who were resource poor and unorganized. This inequitable position clearly worked to the disadvantage of consumers.

So purchasing alliances, even with adequate consumer representation on their boards, are not substitutes for an independent consumer controlled and funded health organization.

A ROLE FOR CONSUMERS

Whether or not such alliances are included in a reform package, a consumer-membership organization is necessary to respond to the concerns of individuals about health care and to involve consumers in the regulatory process. Although the HSA system was generally industry-run and usually ineffective, it was the only opportunity for direct consumer participation in health care planning. Since 1982, consumers have lacked any formal structure through which to protect their rights and promote their interest before regulators and policymakers. A mechanism for such coordination is desperately needed. The establishment of state-wide, democratically-elected, consumer-controlled groups would avoid the pitfalls of the HSA system and provide the mechanism through which consumers could pool their resources and represent their critical interests.

A Consumer Health Insurance Board (CHIB) would fulfill this function. The independence afforded to a voluntarily funded and member-driven organization would allow the CHIB to act as ombudsman to the health care system, and to conduct activities for which the purchasing alliance may neither be funded nor staffed.

Consumer Health Insurance Boards would be established as state-chartered, nonprofit corporations which would be member-funded and administrated through a democratically-elected board of directors. The corporation would be empowered to advise regulatory bodies on behalf of health care consumers of the state, concerning the regulation of providers, carriers, health plans, and alliances. The corporation would assist consumers in the preparation and submission of any claims or disputes in regard to the provision and delivery of health care services and could initiate proceedings or take legal action (with the exception of suits for injury or damages arising from the provision or delivery health care services). The CHIB would also be empowered to represent consumers as a class before any administrative, judicial, or legislative body. In addition, CHIBs would conduct research and surveys regarding health care providers, carriers, health plans, and alliances, and report such information to members and the public at large.

PRECEDENTS

Consumer Health Insurance Boards are modeled in structure and form on Citizens Utility Boards (CUBs). CUBs in Wisconsin, Illinois, Oregon and San Diego have represented the interests of residential and small business utility ratepayers since the early and mid-80's. Their performance has been impressive. The Illinois CUB alone has assisted in saving consumers over $3

97

billion in eight years. The San Diego CUB saved ratepayers nearly $265 million during its first three years of advocacy. And the efforts of the Oregon CUB between 1984 and 1989 saved Oregon ratepayers $318 for every $1 invested in membership fees.

The right to enclose a notice of the CUB's existence with an invitation to join the organization has been crucial to the development of a diverse and substantial membership. For example, the San Diego CUB, known as Utility Consumers Action Network, received 50,000 membership subscriptions in its first nine months and within another year had 160,000 members, out of approximately 4.5 million enclosure recipients. The Illinois CUB, which uses state agency mailings to distribute its enclosures, reports that the average return rate from such enclosures is from one-quarter to one-half percent, bringing in about 4,000 members per month to the CUB.

Illinois was the first state to enact legislation requiring state agencies to include messages concerning the CUB in state mailings. The directive enabling the New York CUB similarly established that the CUB would have the right to insert enclosures in state mailings to New York residents, such as those produced by the Department of Motor Vehicles and the Department of Taxation and Finance. Such enclosures can reach a diverse group of individuals--including those who may not have access to alliances or other health care coverage.

CUB legislation in some states has required the utility companies to enclose a CUB solicitation insert in their mailings. Utility companies have challenged the constitutionality of such legislation. In Pacific Gas & Electric Company v. Public Utilities Commission of California, et. al., 475 U.S. 1, 106 S. Ct. 903 (1986), (hereinafter PG&E), the court found that a private utility company could not be forced to disseminate the newsletter of a private consumer group advocating a political position. The court recognized that states have a broad range of discretion in determining appropriate disclosure requirements, but as Justice Powell noted, there is nothing in current case law to suggest "that the State is equally free to require corporations to carry the messages of third parties, where the messages themselves are biased against or are expressly contrary to the corporation's views." 106 S.Ct. at 911, n.12.

The First Amendment issue raised in this case is avoidable. States can require informational "notice inserts" to be distributed by companies, which would fall within the state's regulatory powers to mandate appropriate disclosure requirements for businesses. Neutrally worded notice inserts, which merely notify consumers of the existence of a CUB and their ability to join, have been used in California since the PG&E decision.

Based on the CUB experience, these enclosures -- in the simple form of a one-page fold-up business reply envelope with an imprinted message -- would piggyback on existing mailings and not increase the usual postage cost of a mailing. The enclosure would inform the recipient of the existence, function, and goals of the Consumer Health Insurance Board and clearly indicate that the CHIB is not sponsored by the government, health care providers, carriers, health plans, nor purchasing alliances. The notice would give the recipient the opportunity to join the organization. The CHIB would pay the cost of producing the enclosures and would reimburse the carrier for any incremental costs associated with inserting the enclosures. Membership subscriptions and private grants would then provide the funding of the CHIB, imposing no compulsory burden on the taxpayers of the state.

CONSUMER HEALTH INSURANCE BOARD MODEL ACT

The empowerment of the American health consumer is crucial to improving the health care system. Accordingly, the creation of Consumer Health Insurance Boards is essential in providing consumers a meaningful role in the process. The attached Consumer Health Insurance Board Model Act would enable a state to set up such an independent, democratic, consumer-member corporation. The model provides a self-funding mechanism for the corporation, including provisions that authorize the CHIB to provide inserts to state agencies, carriers, health plans and alliances in permissible ways. The Consumer Health Insurance Board will enable consumers to communicate with state regulatory agencies and other health care entities to collectively advance the public interest. Congress should consider requiring states to adopt this model as part of any health care reform legislation.

CENTER FOR INSURANCE RESEARCH
11 Stillings Street, 2nd Floor, Boston, MA 02210

CONSUMER HEALTH INSURANCE BOARD MODEL ACT

Table of Contents

Purpose and Intent

The title of this bill shall be known as the CHIB Model Act.

The purpose of this Act is to assist in providing consumers with information concerning the provision and delivery of health care services; to ensure effective consumer representation in the development, operation, and review of public policies and practices affecting the quality and accessibility of health care; and to create an independent mechanism to hold health care [providers, carriers/health plans, and alliances] accountable to consumers. The Act establishes a state-chartered, nonprofit, consumer-membership corporation (a Consumer Health Insurance Board, or CHIB) that is democratically controlled and will gather and disseminate information and represent consumer interests before administrative, judicial and legislative bodies.

It is the intent of this Act to encourage active consumer participation by securing the right of membership to the corporation and by providing simple measures for becoming a member. The consumer interest will be promoted through a board of directors which will be held accountable to such interest through democratic elections and other procedural guarantees.

It is also the intent of this Act to provide an efficient independent funding mechanism for the consumer organization through voluntary contributions, so as not to impose a compulsory burden on the taxpayers of this State.

Section 1.   Definitions

A.   "Campaign contribution" means money, goods, services, or other
benefits paid, made, loaned, given, conferred, or promised, including
but not limited to use of office space, telephones, equipment, staff
services and provisions of meals, drinks, entertainment, services or
transportation made for the purpose of electing a candidate to the board
of directors.

B.   "Carrier" means an insurer, hospital, medical service corporation, or
any other entity responsible for the payment or provision of services
under a health contract.

C.   "Consumer" means an individual who may or may not be a covered
person or purchaser of health care.

D.   "Corporation" means the Consumer Health Insurance Board,
Inc.

E.   "District" means an area comprised of [define as necessary to fit
the geographic and demographic factors of the constituency of the
CHIB. There will be twelve such districts in the state].

Drafting Note: The districts should be enumerated in this Act, and
should be drawn, when possible, according to some existing standard, e.g., two
contiguous state senatorial districts or the federal congressional districts
within the state.

F.   "Enclosure" means a card, leaflet, envelope or combination thereof
furnished by the corporation to a state agency.

G.   "Health care services"

H.   "Health care provider" means a person, facility, or institution licensed,
accredited and/or certified to perform specified health care services, as
required by law.

I.   "Health plan"

J.   The "immediate family" of a person means the person's spouse and
dependent children.

K.   "Notice insert" shall mean a card, leaflet, envelope or combination
thereof furnished by the corporation to [carriers/health plans and
purchasing alliances]. Such insert will inform a consumer of the

existence and purpose of the CHIB, its organization and funding mechanism, the rights of membership, and the process for joining.

**Drafting Note: Neutral notices could be drafted statutorily.

L.   "Purchasing alliance" means a state-chartered, nonprofit organization that provides health coverage purchasing services to member [small] employers in a specified service area.

M.   "State agency" means any department, board, bureau, commission, division, office, council, committee, officer, public benefit corporation or authority, institution or entity of the executive branch of state government.

N.   "Statement" means a written document submitted to the board of directors by a candidate for executive director or the board of directors, in which the information provided by the candidate is sworn, subject to penalty of perjury.

Section 2.   Jurisdiction of the Department of Insurance

Nothing in this Act shall be deemed to limit or conflict with the duties and powers granted to the Commissioner of Insurance under the laws of this State. The corporation established under this Act shall be independent of any state agency or other entity. Violations of this Act shall be subject to the full range of regulatory actions, processes and remedies available to the [Commissioner of Insurance] or other regulatory authority.

Section 3.   Establishment of the Corporation; Membership; Board of Directors

A.   A nonprofit corporation is hereby established to be known as the "Consumer Health Insurance Board" herein referred to as either the "Corporation" or "CHIB".

B.   The membership of the Corporation shall consist of all individuals eighteen (18) years of age or older residing in the state who have contributed to the CHIB the appropriate annual membership fee. The board of directors shall establish an annual membership fee of not less than $5.00, to be adjusted every three years for inflation, and provide for reduced fee membership for low income persons.

C.   The Corporation shall have a board of directors, which shall consist of one elected member from each CHIB voting district, one member appointed by the Governor, one appointed by the Legislature upon the recommendation of the Speaker of the House of

Representatives, and one appointed by the Legislature upon recommendation of the President [Pro Tempore] of the Senate, subject to the requirements of this Act regarding requirements for directors and candidates and election procedures.

D.   The term for all appointed directors shall be two years except that the interim board shall serve until the installation of candidates elected in the first election. One-third of the initially elected directors shall serve one-year terms, one-third of such directors shall serve two-year terms, and one-third of such directors shall serve three-year terms. The initially elected directors shall draw lots to determine the length of their terms. Thereafter, the term of an elected member shall be three years. A member who is appointed to fill an unexpired vacancy after a term has begun serves for the remainder of the term.

E.   No director shall serve more than two consecutive terms. At the end of a term, a member may continue to serve until a successor is appointed, but after three months have expired a successor will be appointed as provided in this Act.

F.   To be eligible for the board of directors, interim or permanent, a member must conform to the following requirements:

    (1)   No person who is not a member of the corporation shall be eligible;

    (2)   No present employee, director, consultant, or attorney of any private or public health care provider, the [Commissioner], nor an immediate family member of any such person shall be eligible;

    (3)   No individual that is in any way affiliated with a licensee of the [Department of Insurance, Public Health] or other licensing authority, including an agent of a licensee, parties receiving compensation from a licensee or agent of a licensee nor an immediate family member of any such person shall be eligible;

    (4)   No person who holds or is a candidate for any other elective public office or who is appointed to hold state or local office shall be eligible;

    (5)   No private individual holding [five] percent or more interest in a [provider, carrier/health plan, or alliance]; or owning or being employed by a company who receives more than [five] percent of

its gross revenue from a [provider, carrier/health plan, or alliance] or any combination of the above shall be eligible.

**Drafting note: This provision attempts to exclude any individual with a financial interest or economic stake in a [provider, carrier/health plan, or alliance] from membership to the board of directors. Some revision may be necessary.

G.   Before the first general election for directors, the Corporation shall be managed as follows:

    (1)   Within 90 days of the effective date of this Act, the Governor shall appoint five individuals to the interim board of directors, and the Speaker of the House of Representatives and the President [Pro Tempore] of the Senate shall each appoint five individuals to the interim Board of Directors. The interim directors should be representative of each of the following categories of organizations: consumer; labor; civil rights; neighborhood; elderly; and lower income, including legal service organizations. In making such appointments, consideration should also be given to the state's geographical, ethnic, gender, and workforce diversity.

    (2)   Within 120 days of the effective date of this Act the interim board of directors shall organize the CHIB; inform health care consumers of and solicit their membership in the CHIB; elect officers; employ such staff as are necessary; solicit funds; and establish procedures for democratic election of members of the board of directors not inconsistent with this Act.

    (3)   Not more than 60 days after the membership of the CHIB reaches 20,000 or .5 percent of the population (as determined in the last census), whichever amount is less, with at least [100] members in each CHIB district, the interim board of directors shall set a date for the first general election of directors and shall so notify every member. The date set for elections shall be not less than four months nor more than eight months after such notification. The interim board shall oversee the election campaign and tally the votes.

    (4)   Not more than 30 days after the first general election the interim board shall install the elected and newly appointed directors, and carry out all duties necessary to transfer leadership to the new board.

(5)   The Corporation shall not represent the membership before any administrative, judicial or legislative body before such time as the first elected board of directors is installed, except in situations where the authority of the interim board or the existence of the CHIB is challenged. The interim board of directors shall not be authorized to carry out the powers and duties of the Corporation or board of directors enumerated in this Act except such duties imposed by this subsection.

(6)   Members of the interim board of directors shall be reimbursed for actual, reasonable expenses.

(7)   The interim period will count as one term.

H.   A candidate for election to the board of directors must comply with the following election procedures:

(1)   Not later than 90 days prior to the election, a candidate shall submit a statement of intent to run for the board of directors, and shall therein affirm that he or she complies with the eligibility requirements of this Act.

(2)   Not later than 90 days prior to the election, a candidate shall file with the board of directors a statement of financial interest upon a form provided by the board. The statement of financial interest, which shall be open for public inspection, shall include the following information: the occupation, employer and position of the candidate; a list of all fiduciary relationships, corporate and organizational directorships, or other offices held in the past three years by the candidate; certification that no one in his or her immediate family is employed by, or an agent or representative of a [provider, carrier/health plan, or alliance]; and such other information as the board of directors shall require candidates to disclose.

(3)   Not later than 10 days after receiving the statement of intent and the statement of financial interest, the board of directors shall notify the candidate that his or her candidacy has been certifed by the board if the candidate meets the eligibility requirements of this Act.

(4)   Not later than 60 days prior to the election, a candidate shall submit to the board of directors, on a form to be provided by the board, a statement concerning his or her personal background and positions on issues relating to the regulation of health care

[providers, carriers/health plans, and alliances], or the
operations of the Corporation.

(5)   No candidate may spend more than two thousand dollars or the
postage cost of two one-ounce first-class mailings to each CHIB
member in the candidate's district, whichever amount is greater,
on campaign expenditures from four months prior to the
election, through the date of the election.

(6)   No candidate may accept more than [two hundred] dollars in
campaign contributions from any one contributor during the
year preceding the date of the election.

(7)   No candidate shall accept campaign contributions from any
present employee, director, consultant, attorney, or accountant of
any health care provider, carrier/health plan, or alliance, any
private individual or entity that is in any way affiliated with a
licensee of the [Department of Insurance or Public Health], or
other licensing authority, an agent of a licensee, or a party
receiving compensation from a licensee or agent of a licensee.

(8)   Each candidate for election to the board of directors shall keep
complete records of all contributions of fifty dollars or more to
the candidate's campaign made during the year preceding the
date of the election. Not later than 30 days after the election,
each candidate shall submit to the board of directors, on a form
provided by the board of directors, an accurate statement of
campaign contributions accepted and campaign expenses
incurred. Such records shall be available for inspection by the
public.

(9)   If the board of directors determines that a candidate's campaign
expenses have exceeded the limits contained in this Act, the
candidate shall be disqualified and may be required to pay the
expenses incurred by the Corporation in mailing the candidate's
statement of personal background and position.

(10)   No candidate may use any campaign contribution for any
purpose other than campaign expenditures. Any remaining
campaign funds shall be donated to the CHIB within 20 days
after the election.

Elections will be held annually in the one-third of voting districts in
which a representative's term will expire. Elections and installment of
directors will take place as follows:

(1)   Not later than 30 days before the date fixed for a special or general election, the board of directors shall send to each member an official ballot listing all candidates for the board of directors from their district who have complied with all the requirements of this Act, each such candidate's statement of financial interests, and each such candidate's statement of personal background and position.

(2)   Each consumer who is a member on the thirtieth day preceding an election may cast a vote by returning his or her official ballot, properly marked, to the principal office of the Corporation by eight p.m. of the date fixed for the election. Voting shall be by secret ballot. The candidate receiving the greatest number of votes in each district shall be declared elected.

(3)   Each general election of directors other than the first election of directors shall be held not less than eleven months and not more than thirteen months after the last preceding general election. The date of such election shall be fixed by the board of directors at least four months in advance of the date chosen for the election.

(4)   Within 30 days after the election, the president of the board of directors shall install in office all elected candidates who meet the qualifications prescribed in this Act.

(5)   The [Commissioner, Office of the Attorney General, or Elections Division] shall oversee the fairness of elections and certify compliance with the procedures enumerated in this Act.

J.   When a director dies, resigns, is disqualified, or otherwise vacates office, the board of directors shall select, within three months, a successor from the same district as such director for the remainder of the director's term of office. Any director may nominate any person meeting the requirements of this Act. The board of directors shall select the successor from among those nominated, by a two-thirds majority of the remaining directors present and voting. The successor shall be installed in office by the president of the board of directors within 30 days after the office has been vacated.

K.   The board of directors shall have the following duties:

(1)   To prescribe rules for the conduct of elections and election campaigns not inconsistent with this Act;

(2)   To prescribe rules and procedures for the appointment of directors, and for installment of elected and appointed directors;

(3)   To establish the policies of the Corporation regarding appearances before administrative, judicial and legislative bodies, and regarding other activities which the Corporation has the authority to perform under this Act;

(4)   To establish appropriate procedures for closing meetings for the purposes of discussing legislative and litigation strategies or matters of personnel;

(5)   To make and maintain all reports and studies compiled by the CHIB pursuant to this Act available for public inspection during regular business hours;

(6)   To maintain up-to-date membership rolls, including a list of the current membership by district, available for inspection by any member upon request;

(7)   To establish procedures governing the reimbursement of directors for actual reasonable expenses incurred by them in the performance of their duties;

(8)   To keep minutes, books and records which shall relect all the acts and transactions of the board of directors which shall be open to examination by any member, with the exception of closed sessions in which the minutes may be sealed;

(9)   To ensure that the Corporation's books are audited by an independent certified public accountant at least once each fiscal year, and to make the audit available to the general public;

(10) To prepare, as soon as practicable but not later than four months after the close of the Corporations's fiscal year, an annual report of the Corporation's financial and substantive operations which shall be made available for public inspection;

(11) To conduct an annual membership meeting and therein report to the membership on the past and projected activities and policies of the CHIB. In addition, the CHIB shall sponsor on behalf of each director at least one meeting per year in each CHIB electoral district;

(12) To annually elect officers;

(13) To employ an executive director, and establish policies for employment and removal. The executive director may employ and direct staff as necessary to carry out the provisions of this Act;

(14) To hold regular board meetings open to the public at least once every four months on such dates and at such places as it may determine. Special meetings may be called by the president of the board of directors or by at least one-quarter of the directors upon at least five days' notice. One-half of the directors plus one shall constitute a quorum. Additional meetings of the Board shall also be open to the public except where circumstances require closed sessions and procedures to close a meeting have been followed;

(15) To carry out all other duties and responsibilities imposed upon the CHIB and the board of directors and to exercise all powers necessary to accomplish the purposes of this Act.

L. The executive director hired by the board of directors shall be subject to the conflict of interest provision as well as the restriction on holding any other public office in subsection (F) of this section. The executive director may not be a candidate for the Board of Directors while serving as executive director. All candidates for executive director must submit a statement of financial interest as is required of board members and the executive director shall be required to file such a statement annually. In addition, the executive director must covenant not to take a position as an agent, representative, licensee or employee of the [Department of Insurance or Public Health], or any health care [provider, carrier/health plan, or alliance] for one year after serving as executive director.

M. All directors except the executive director will receive not more than [$2000] annually in compensation and will be reimbursed for actual reasonable expenses incurred in the performance of their duties.

Section 4.   Funding System for the Corporation

A. The CHIB shall be funded by voluntary donations from its members and through other grants and donations, including intervenor compensation funds for which it might be eligible or litigation awards, subject to the restriction that no gift, loan, grant or other aid shall be accepted from any health care [provider, carrier/health plan, or alliance] or any employee, director, consultant, attorney or any agent or other representative of any health care [provider, carrier/health plan, or alliance], nor any private individual or entity that is in any way affiliated with a licensee of the [Department of Insurance], including an agent of a licensee or a party receiving compensation from a licensee or agent of a licensee.

B. The CHIB shall prepare an enclosure soliciting voluntary membership contributions which shall be furnished to any state agency and included, upon the request of the CHIB, in any mailing by that agency to at least [1000] individuals, subject to the following requirements:

   (1) Upon furnishing any state agency the enclosure permitted by this subsection, the CHIB shall certify that the enclosure is neither false nor misleading.

   (2) If the agency finds the enclosure to be false or misleading, it must notify the CHIB and provide opportunity for the CHIB to correct the enclosure expeditiously. If the CHIB refuses to modify the enclosure, the state agency may submit its complaint in writing to the [Commissioner], who shall review the enclosure within 30 days, and may disapprove the enclosure if it is false or misleading. Upon submitting its complaint, the agency may proceed with regularly scheduled mailings until notified by the [Commissioner].

   (3) The CHIB will reimburse the state agency for the reasonable incremental postage and handling costs incurred as a result of compliance with this subsection, provided that an itemized accounting of the additional costs is received prior to the costs being incurred.

C. The CHIB shall prepare and furnish any [purchasing alliance] operating in the state a notice insert soliciting voluntary membership contributions which shall be included, upon the request of the CHIB, in any mailing by such alliance to at least [1000] individuals, subject to the following requirements:

   (1) The notice insert must contain neutral language intended to inform a consumer of the existence and purpose of the CHIB, its organization and funding mechanism, the rights of membership, and the process for joining. The CHIB shall certify that the notice is neither biased nor expressly contradictory to the views of the [purchasing alliance].

   (2) No [purchasing alliance] is required to enclose a notice insert in its mailings more than [four] times per year.

(3) If the [purchasing alliance] objects to the language of an insert because it is biased or expressly contradictory to the views of the [purchasing alliance], it must notify the CHIB and provide opportunity for the CHIB to correct the enclosure expeditiously. If the CHIB refuses to modify the insert the [alliance] may submit its complaint in writing to the [Commissioner]; who shall review the insert within 30 days, and may disapprove the insert if it contains biased or expressly contradictory language. Upon submitting its complaint, the [alliance] may proceed with regularly scheduled mailings until notified by the [Commissioner].

(4) The CHIB will reimburse the [purchasing alliance] for the reasonable incremental postage and handling costs incurred as a result of compliance with this subsection, provided that an itemized accounting of the additional costs is received prior to the costs being incurred.

D. The CHIB shall prepare and furnish any [carrier/health plan] operating in the state a notice insert soliciting voluntary membership contributions which shall be included, upon the request of the CHIB, in any mailing by such [carrier/health plan] to at least [1000] individuals, subject to the following requirements:

(1) The notice insert must contain neutral language intended to inform a consumer of the existence and purpose of the CHIB, its organization and funding mechanism, the rights of membership, and the process for joining. The CHIB shall certify that the notice is neither biased nor expressly contradictory to the views of the [carrier/health plan].

(2) No [carrier/health plan] is required to enclose a notice insert in its mailings more than [four] times per year.

(3) If the [carrier/health plan] objects to the language of an insert because it is biased or expressly contradictory to the views of the [carrier/health plan], it must notify the CHIB and provide opportunity for the CHIB to correct the enclosure expeditiously. If the CHIB refuses to modify the insert the [carrier/health plan] may submit its complaint in writing to the [Commissioner], who shall review the insert within 30 days, and may disapprove the insert if it contains biased or expressly contradictory language. Upon submitting its complaint, the agency may proceed with
· regularly scheduled mailings until notified by the [Commissioner].

(4) The CHIB will reimburse the [carrier/health plan] for the reasonable incremental postage and handling costs incurred as a result of compliance with this subsection, provided that an itemized accounting of the additional costs is received prior to the costs being incurred.

Section 5. Powers and Duties of the Corporation

The Consumer Health Insurance Board shall have the following powers and duties:

A. Advise the [Commissioner of Insurance and Secretary of Public Health] on behalf of health care consumers of the State regarding policies and practices in the provision and delivery of health care services and regulation of providers, carriers/health plans and alliances;

B. Educate and assist consumers as individuals or collectively concerning preparation and submission of claims or disputes to the Commissioner or any other entity in regard to provision and delivery of health care services;

C. Represent and promote the interests of consumers individually or as a class before any administrative or judicial body, and before any local, state, and federal legislative or policymaking bodies;

D. Initiate, maintain, or participate in any proceeding related to health care services which affects the interests of consumers, for which it shall have standing, including standing to bring suit, except that the CHIB shall not represent any person in any action for compensation for injury or damages arising from any provision of health care services or health insurance;

E. Conduct and support research, surveys, conferences and public information activities concerning health care services, [providers, carriers/health plans and alliances];

F. Develop proposals to improve the delivery and quality of health care services;

G. Inform consumers about the existence of the CHIB, including procedures for obtaining membership, and to take affirmative measures to encourage membership by low and moderate income and minority consumers;

H. Perform all acts necessary or expedient for the administration of its affairs and the attainment of its purpose.

Section 6.   Construction and Severability

A.   This Act, being necessary for the welfare of the state and its inhabitants, shall be liberally construed to effect its purposes.

B.   Nothing in this Act shall be construed to limit the right of any individual, group, or class of individuals to initiate, intervene in, or otherwise participate in any proceeding before any administrative, judicial, or legislative bodies; nor to require any petition or notification to the CHIB as a condition precedent to any such right; nor to relieve any agency, court or other public body of any obligation, or affect its discretion to permit intervention or participation by a consumer or group of consumers in any proceeding or activity; nor to limit the right of any individual or individuals to obtain administrative or judicial review.

C.   If any clause, sentence, paragraph or part of this Act or the application thereof be adjudged by a court of competent jurisdiction to be invalid, such judgment shall not affect, impair or invalidate the remainder, and the application thereof, but shall be confined in its operation to the clause, sentence, paragraph or part thereof directly involved in the controversy in which such judgment shall have been rendered.

Mr. TOWNS. Mr. Wetzell.

Mr. WETZELL. Thank you, Mr. Chairman.

My name is Steve Wetzell. I am executive director of the Business Health Care Action Group, a buying coalition headquartered in the Twin Cities, purchasing health care on behalf of about a quarter of a million employees, retirees and their families over a 5-State region.

And the first thing I would like to do is to go on record, Mr. Chair, as advocating Federal reform this year. Our employers are large. They are self-insured. A number of large self-insured companies have gone on record saying there isn't a problem. We believe there needs to be Federal reform, and we believe it needs to be this year, and we want to go on record as saying that.

We also believe that we are demonstrating that the large employers can play a constructive role in market reform. Not only for the people that we insure; namely, our employees, our retirees and their families, but for the broader community. If we set the standards to drive providers and health plans to compete based on quality and cost containment rather than ability to underwrite and select best risk in the community, we believe that benefits the entire community, not just the people we insure.

We have 21 member companies. We are all self-insured. We all bear our own risk. It is a critical point we want to make that when employers are allowed to self-insure it does give them significant incentives to buy and control costs and improve qualities, because they have a direct vested interest in reforming the market that they buy in when they bear their own risk. Although we do believe that it is appropriate for the Federal Government to set standards to limit the size of an employer that elects to self-insure so there isn't abuse of the self-insurance system.

We have negotiated a common health plan. All 21 companies have the same standard set of benefits. We advocate a Federal benefit package to provide consumer protection.

We do not favor State-by-State packages for a couple of reasons. We believe it will confuse consumers because it is interstate commerce. Consumers move across State lines. They commute across State lines. And we fear that if standard benefit sets are given to the States it may get politicized and we may not make rational policy decisions on standard benefits.

We have issued our contracts to providers based primarily on the assumption that providers improve quality cost containment will automatically follow. We have not negotiated discounts. Our contracts are awarded based on provider commitment to working collectively within organized systems of care to define what is the best practice standard for medicine, eliminate ways to measure patient outcomes and continuously improve the process of delivering care.

And we are already seeing signs in our process where we may be able to eliminate as many as 15 percent of the office visits that currently occur in our managed care plans in the community and actually improve the quality of care in the process.

So, our philosophy is that the key to cost containment is quality improvement and that you don't have to reduce quality in exchange for controlling costs.

We operate our coalition with a staff of two full-time professionals and one part-time administrative staffperson, and the resources to support the coalition's work are primarily provided through volunteer time from our member employers.

Our annual budget is less than one half of 1 percent of total expenditures for the member companies on the health plan we offer.

The written testimony that we provided gives our results and I won't brag about them today, but we have had pretty impressive results so far. The key point we want to make is we believe that our results are not at the expense of businesses and purchasers in our community that aren't in the coalition. We do not actively engage in cost shifting by negotiating discounts.

Our focus is on making providers accountable, to define what care is necessary not only for the people that we cover but for every patient that walks in their door. And we believe that that is a constructive role for the community that makes the system more efficient, will make it more accessible without creating cost shifting between the big powerful purchasers and the smaller employers and those individuals buying in the individual market that don't have the clout that we have.

We believe that Federal standards should be established to regulate the activities of purchasing cooperatives, and we strongly favor Federal standards over State standards. I agree with Mr. Adkins' testimony, with the exception that we do strongly fear excessive power given to the States largely because the stakeholders that I represent are interstate employers that do business in all 50 States and the District of Columbia, and we do prefer Federal standards over State standards.

We think cooperatives should be voluntary and competing, not mandatory or monopolistic. Because health care consumption and purchasing isn't based on State boundaries, we do think Federal standards are appropriate.

We believe that rules should maintain incentives for cooperatives to improve quality and cost. That it shouldn't just be a price issue. That there should be standards that assess our ability to buy based on quality also. That it should not be purely driven by what kind of premiums or fees we can negotiate with our providers. There has to be accountability for quality of the products we offer.

We believe that both self-insured and insured models should be permitted under the Federal rules. A technical issue that we probably can't get into a lot of detail today, but current Federal rules under ERISA, the law that protects multi-State employers from State regulation, inhibit us from negotiating risk-sharing arrangements through direct contracting with providers, and that is a real barrier to innovation. So, we would like the Federal Government to consider rules that would allow self-insured employers and coalitions to directly contract with providers entering into risk-sharing arrangements without falling under State regulation.

Underwriting reform is essential. Cooperatives cannot survive if the insurance industry continues to compete based on its ability to pick healthy people to insure. So, I think it is a given, and we are encouraged that both parties and Congress and the administration seem to be reaching a consensus that underwriting reform is absolutely essential as a cornerstone to health care reform, and we advocate that.

A concern we do have is the acceleration of anti-managed care rules at the State level and discussion at the Federal level. Any willing provider is one of those issues that is being discussed.

We want a contract with our providers on behalf of our employees and our retirees and their families based on their commitment to quality. And, if we have rules that mandate that we contract with every provider that is willing to agree to a specified fee schedule, we can't control the most critical part of the equation, and that is rewarding providers for quality with more market share. So, we would like to see Federal rules that prohibit States from passing laws that limit our ability to negotiate with providers based on quality and cost.

We believe that it is appropriate to have rules to protect consumers against cooperatives that are organized to cherry-pick risk. And I think Mr. Adkins testified to this very well. We fear that the cooperatives will start doing what the insurance companies have done historically and very well. They will contract around the high risk populations, around the minority populations, and we are not going to solve the problem. So, rules should be established that require the cooperatives contract with providers throughout a specified geographic area to eliminate that kind of game playing both in the insurance industry and among these cooperatives and alliances.

And we also believe in strong consumer protection. Cooperatives should have solvency requirements to make sure they have adequate reserves to pay for the promise to cover the people that enroll in most cooperatives. There should be rights to appeal for consumers. And there should be a standard benefit set at the Federal level so consumers have a floor that they can't fall below and they know what their protection is.

Thank you, Mr. Chairman.

Mr. TOWNS. Thank you very much for your testimony.

[The prepared statement of Mr. Wetzell follows:]

Highlights of Testimony of the Business Health Care Action Group
Human Resources and Intergovernmental Relations Subcommittee
of the Committee on Government Operations
June 30, 1994

Mr. Steve Wetzell
Executive Director of the Business Health Care Action Group
Minneapolis, Minnesota

Facts regarding the Business Health Care Action Group (BHCAG)

- Minneapolis/St Paul group purchasing organization.

- 21 self-insured employers who have developed health plan offered to 250,000 employees, retirees and their families in Minnesota, western Wisconsin, eastern North and South Dakota, and northern Iowa - member companies include:

Bemis Company, Inc.	Medtronic
Cargill, Inc.	Minnegasco
Carlson Companies	Minnesota Mutual
Cenex	Northern States Power Company
Ceridian Corporation	Norwest Corporation
Dayton Hudson Corporation	Pillsbury Company
First Bank System	Rosemount, Inc.
General Mills, Inc.	SUPERVALU INC.
Honeywell Inc.	Tennant
IDS Financial Services, Inc.	3M
Land O' Lakes	

- Member employers provide health care coverage for more than 1.5 million Americans in all 50 states and District of Columbia.

- Annual health care expenditures in the region exceed $500 million and $1.5 billion nationwide.

- Reform is based on improved quality, increased provider accountability and competition, increased consumer knowledge and responsibility, and enhanced efficiency of the health care system.

- ERISA preemption and freedom from state-by-state regulation has encouraged this innovative approach to develop systems that improve quality and access while containing costs

Key features of BHCAG reform activity

- Common health plan design and administration effective 1/1/93.

- Self-insured "Point-of-Service" benefit design that includes comprehensive major medical, preventive care, mental health, substance abuse and pharmacy benefits.

- Vertically integrated network of contracted providers which offers consumers freedom to choose physicians while offering financial incentives to use the most cost effective, high quality health care professionals.

- Administrative services provided through local health plan.

- Health care professionals and employers working together to define and measure quality standards, assess new technologies, and develop and offer consumer education courses at the work site.

- Plan offered to eligible employees, retirees and dependents of member employers.

- Coalition governed by member employer Human Resource executives.

- Coalition staff of two full time professionals and one part time administrative assistant - 1994 coalition budget is $500,000.

Results

- 100,000 enrolled members in five states.

- First year savings of 11% compared to other managed care products in Minnesota. Cost about 30% below national average.

- Savings due to improved efficiency and reduced utilization which benefits all purchasers, not due to additional discounts which would be cost shifted to other payers.

- 1993 average cost of $2,500 per employee - average family size of 2.1 people means average annual cost of $1,200 per covered life.

- Administrative costs are 8% to 10% of total plan expenses, coalition budget less than 1% of total plan cost.

- Current annual rate of increase of 4% - 5%, which is significantly less than state expenditure targets.

- No increase in administrative costs from 1993 to 1994.

General Public Policy Issues Pertaining to Purchasing Cooperatives

- Cooperatives should be voluntary and competing.

- Health care consumption/purchasing is not based on state boundaries - federal guidelines preferred over state-by-state regulation.

- Rules should maintain incentives for Cooperatives to improve quality and contain cost.

- Both self-insured and insured models should be permitted.

- Federal rules to allow multi-state self-insured employers and cooperatives to negotiate risk sharing contracts with providers without falling under state regulation.

- Underwriting reform essential to support formation of Cooperatives for smaller businesses.

- "Anti-managed Care" rules should be prohibited to allow Cooperatives to contract with providers and plans based on quality and cost.

- Rules appropriate to protect against Cooperatives which "cherry-pick" risk.

- Consumer protection through solvency requirements, rights to appeal, and standard benefits sets.

Testimony of Business Health Care Action Group
Human Resources and Intergovernmental Relations Subcommittee
of the Committee on Government Operations
June 30, 1994

Mr. Steve Wetzell
Executive Director of the Business Health Care Action Group
Minneapolis, Minnesota

Mr Chairman and members of the committee, I am Steve Wetzell, executive director of the Business Health Care Action Group. On behalf of our 21 member employers, I would like to express our sincere appreciation for the opportunity to testify today on our experience operating a health care purchasing cooperative

Who We Are

Prior to addressing regulations of health care purchasing cooperatives, it may be helpful to provide some background information about the Business Health Care Action Group (BHCAG) and how it benefits the regional and national health care market. The BHCAG strongly believes that the private sector can and should play a significant role in solving our nation's health care problems. We believe we have developed a model for private sector based reform that can improve the quality and access to care and control costs without cost shifting to other health care purchasers.

BHCAG membership currently includes twenty one, large self-insured employers. Our member companies include:

Bemis Company, Inc.	Medtronic, Inc.
Cargill, Inc.	Minnegasco
Carlson Companies	Minnesota Mutual
Cenex	Norwest Corporation
Ceridian Corporation	Northern States Power Company
Dayton Hudson Corporation	The Pillsbury Company
First Bank System	Rosemount Inc.
General Mills, Inc.	SUPERVALU INC.
Honeywell Inc.	TENNANT
IDS Financial Services, Inc.	3M
Land O' Lakes	

This coalition has developed a self-insured health plan which member companies offer to more than 250,000 people in Minnesota, western Wisconsin, eastern North and South Dakota, and northern Iowa. The employers and their employees spend about $500 million annually on health care services within the region. Collectively, the member employers of the BHCAG provide health care coverage for more than 1.5 million Americans residing in all 50 states and the District of Columbia at an annual expense of about $1 5 billion.

We have agreed to a common comprehensive benefit plan, contracted with the same network of health care providers, and negotiated a long term contract with regional health care providers which contains aggressive quality and cost guarantees

The coalition has a staff of two full time professionals and one part time administrative assistant. The 1994 budget to support direct coalition expenditures is $500,000 The BHCAG is incorporated as a for-profit entity, although the coalition has no intent to create "profits" from its activities Although a not-for-profit structure was preferred, a for-profit structure was established because this was the most cost effective method to create a corporate structure without imposing an additional legal and administrative burden to demonstrate the organization would qualify as a non-profit entity The coalition's budget is supported by cash contributions from its member employers In addition, significant volunteer resources are provided by member employers to support coalition activities. The coalition is governed by a board of directors made up of senior human resource professionals representing the member employers

Our primary goal is to provide our employees, retirees and their families with high quality, affordable health care by creating provider accountability for quality health outcomes and defining the care that is necessary to treat patients in the most cost effective manner We also are using this model to develop similar competing health plans in the region and across the country We believe we have demonstrated our ability to meet these objectives without cost shifting to other purchasers or requiring the burden of state regulatory requirements.

We believe that employers who purchase health care can use their influence as a catalyst for market based progressive reforms, not only for those to whom we provide coverage, but also for the community as a whole This approach to delivery system reform will benefit consumers, purchasers, and providers who deliver high quality, cost effective care. We believe that the experience gained through this initiative can be applied to health care reform on a broader basis.

What We Have Accomplished

Participating BHCAG companies began introducing a new health care plan designed around these principles effective January 1, 1993. Our results have been impressive

- Although most BHCAG member employers offer several other health plans to their employees and retirees, including HMOs, PPOs and traditional fee-for-service indemnity plans, more than 100,000 of 250,000 eligible employees, retirees and their dependents have voluntarily enrolled in the coalition's health plan.

- The coalition has grown from 14 to 21 employers with no money spent on "marketing" the coalition to other employers in the community.

- The plan offers comprehensive benefits The plan generally provides 100% coverage after reasonable copayments are made by plan participants when contracted providers are used. In addition to comprehensive coverage for catastrophic health care needs, the plan covers preventive care, mental health, substance abuse and prescription drugs.

- The plan protects the members right to choose their own physician while offering financial incentives to use the most cost effective, high quality providers

- The cost to cover each employee in 1993 was only $2,500. With each employee having an average family size of 2 1 lives, the average cost for each covered member of the plan was $1,200.

- Overall costs were reduced 11% in 1993 compared to similar HMO products currently available in the region. Cost reductions were largely due to reduced utilization and improved efficiency, not due to provider 'discounts' which would result in cost shifting to other purchasers.

- Administrative costs were 8% - 10% of total plan costs, including the costs to conduct coalition activities, and will not increase in 1994 The coalition's budget was less than 1% of total health care expenditures for the health plan.

- The annual rate of increase in plan cost is 4% - 5%, significantly below recently passed state targets on health care cost increases which apply to state regulated purchasers.

- Contracted providers have developed and agreed to follow common practice standards to assure consistent, high quality care for plan participants.

- Contracted providers have agreed to and are providing data to measure patient outcomes to document and improve the quality of care

- Contracted providers and purchasers are jointly assessing new medical technologies to assure that resources are allocated to procedures and medical devices with a proven benefit to patients.

- Contracted providers have developed a prototype for an automated medical record to facilitate the collection of data to measure patient outcomes and more efficiently gather information to support quality improvement and cost containment.

- Contracted providers and BHCAG member employers are developing health education classes which will be offered at the worksites of coalition members.

- An annual member satisfaction survey will be conducted to solicit consumer feedback and maintain accountability for the overall value of the health plan to its participants.

- Efforts are underway to create an insured product for small employers to allow businesses of all sizes to participate in and benefit from coalition activities.

- Additional coalition sponsored plans will be developed and compete with the initial plan.

- Three other coalitions have adapted our model to stimulate similar market changes in Dayton, Ohio, Rockford, Illinois and Des Moines, Iowa. Employers in San Francisco, St. Louis, Baton Rouge, Grand Forks, Michigan and Phoenix have requested information on our activities and are considering similar private sector initiatives modeled after our project.

- Health care providers from New York, Oregon, Arizona, California, Washington, Illinois, Michigan, Ohio, Kansas, Wisconsin, and Texas have requested information regarding our purchasing initiative to begin preparing for similar private sector purchaser expectations in those states

The Minnesota Health Care Market

"Managed Care" is not a new concept in the Twin Cities of Minneapolis and St. Paul. Driven by the demands of private purchasers, organized systems of care have been evolving for many years.

At the time the BHCAG decided to engage in a group purchasing initiative, the market was dominated by state regulated Health Maintenance Organizations (HMOs) and Preferred Provider Organizations (PPOs). It is estimated that about 70% of the residents of the greater Minneapolis/St. Paul urban area are currently enrolled in various forms of 'managed care' health plans featuring contracted relationships between providers and insurance carriers or health maintenance organizations. In addition, the market has significant numbers of large group medical practices and multi-specialty clinics. Health care costs in the Twin Cities are about 18% below the national average largely due to the impact of managed care products and organized systems of care in the market place which have been created in response to private sector purchaser demands

In spite of this high penetration of managed care products, the member employers of the BHCAG observed that there was need for improvement in the quality and efficiency of the health care system Meaningful quality data about competing health plans and provider networks was not available to consumers or purchasers Because providers were contracted with multiple managed care and insurance vendors, there was no real incentive at the individual hospital or clinic level to compete for patients based on quality and cost.

In addition, managed care contracts with providers were largely based on discount fee for service arrangements. While addressing unit pricing, this approach did not get at the issue of quality or ineffective and unnecessary care In addition, like Medicare/Medicaid reimbursement policies over the past several years, the extensive use of discounts in managed care products to generate "savings" resulted in significant cost shifting by health care providers within the Twin Cities market to participants in non-managed care (i e - indemnity) health plans. Medical inflation rates, while running well below the national average, still exceeded real growth in the economy

In this environment, BHCAG decided that purchasers, working directly with preferred providers in a long term arrangement, could improve on the current health care delivery system.

Recently, the Minnesota legislature has passed a series of laws which will apply to the Minnesota health care market. Although the theory upon which the Minnesota legislation was based would support a competitive, relatively unregulated market place, the state legislature and the administration appear to moving more and more towards a highly regulatory approach with numerous rules which would limit the creativity and innovation of the private sector if it fell under the new rules

As multi-state employers who are engaged in a regional collective purchasing activity, the member employers of the BHCAG strongly endorse federal standards which regulate purchasing alliances and self-insured plans over conflicting and oftentimes anti-competitive rules established on a state-by-state basis.

Federal Regulation of Health Care Purchasing Cooperatives

As advocates of a competitive approach to improve quality, access and affordability of health care, the BHCAG supports the creation of a regulatory environment which stimulates the development of voluntary, competing health care purchasing cooperatives. We believe that government or private sector operated purchasing monopolies will not do the best job of improving quality or containing costs However, certain general rules are appropriate to assure that competing, voluntary cooperatives operate in a way which serves the public interest.

Because health care purchasing is an interstate enterprise, we advocate federal rules to regulate the activities of purchasing cooperatives. These rules should maintain incentives for these cooperatives to improve quality, access and cost. For example, if rules required pure "community rating," cooperatives would not have incentives to improve quality or contain cost Rules should allow cooperatives to accept responsibility for their own health care costs as long as they don't intentionally limit membership only to "healthy" people.

To protect the public against "cherry picking" of healthy risk by cooperatives, federal rules should prohibit them from establishing criteria for membership based on the health status of an employer's population. Further, to assure cooperatives do not avoid serving parts of the community with known high risk populations, the cooperatives should be required develop or contract with health plans which provide access to care throughout a defined geographic region. As long as private cooperatives demonstrate compliance with these general rules, further regulation of their membership criteria is unnecessary

Insurance underwriting reform is essential to support the development of private health care purchasing cooperatives Currently, insurance companies can undermine the development of employer governed purchasing cooperatives by offering favorable premiums to businesses with healthy populations This leaves only high risk groups who might have an interest in forming a purchasing pool. Ultimately, the pool goes into a "death spiral" as insurance companies continue to "buy off" the best risk from the pool by offering low premiums to those businesses with healthy employees. To support the creation of voluntary employer governed purchasing pools, federal rules should significantly limit the extent to which insurance companies can vary premiums for individual employers based on the health status of employees, retirees and their families.

To maintain the leverage of cooperatives to negotiate the best contracts with providers and health plans based on quality, access and cost, states should be prohibited from imposing "anti-managed care" rules such as "any willing provider" provisions. Many states have passed or are considering rules which require health plans to contract with any provider who is willing to agree to set prices and quality standards. This type of rule destroys the ability of purchasers to negotiate aggressively with competing providers and health plans to improve quality, access and cost standards within the community. Federal rules should prohibit this kind of anti-competitive regulation not only for purchasing cooperatives, but for all health care purchasers and plans.

Many large employers prefer to bear their own risk rather than paying a profit to an insurance company to do it for them Federal rules should continue to allow larger employers to self-insure their covered population. In addition, because current federal rules generally limit the ability of self-insured employers and cooperatives to negotiate directly with providers without falling under state regulation, federal rules should be created which allow coalitions made up of self-insured employers to negotiate risk sharing arrangements with providers without being subject to state regulation.

Certain federal rules are also appropriate to protect consumers covered by health plans offered through purchasing cooperatives Federal rules which define the rights to appeal coverage decisions are recommended. In addition, if cooperatives elect to bear their own risk, solvency requirements should be created to protect consumers from under funded plans offered through purchasing alliances A standard set of benefits established at the federal level would also be appropriate

Thank you for offering this opportunity to share our opinions and concerns regarding the critical public policy issue of health care reform. As an active example of a purchasing alliance, the member employers of the Business Health Care Action Group would welcome the opportunity to continue to share our experience as Congress and the Administration continue to move towards a national framework designed to improve quality, access and affordability of health care for all Americans.

Mr. TOWNS. We have also been joined by Congressman Mica from Florida.

Let me begin by saying it is my understanding that Florida use existing social service areas as the boundary lines for your alliances. Is that right?

Mr. COOK. Yes, sir, that is correct. And they do roughly correspond with the SMSA areas of the State.

Mr. TOWNS. That means that some alliances have a much higher percentage of poor people than other alliances. Is that true?

Mr. COOK. No, sir. The fact of the matter is, to the extent that they are roughly—they roughly correspond to the geographical area that they represent, and frankly, I don't think that we have—well, let me try to answer your question.

Mr. TOWNS. No poor people in Florida.

Mr. COOK. No. There are a lot of poor people in Florida, but they are roughly distributed around the State. Miami has more people and therefore more poor people, but proportionately Miami has a number of rich people as well.

No, I wouldn't say that they have a disproportionate share, any one alliance district has a disproportionate share of poor people roughly corresponding with its regular population.

Mr. TOWNS. I guess the next question probably would be then, based on your answer, is how do you prevent insurers from redlining alliances? I mean how do you prevent redlining.

Mr. COOK. Well, sir, they can't redline. They have to insure everybody in that county. OK? So they have to provide—for instance, in Dade County they can't choose to insure one part of Dade County and not insure all of Dade County. They have to insure the entire county as a whole. So, if they offer a plan in a county, they have to offer it all over the county to anyone in that county.

So, in Dade County, for instance, there are areas of Miami Beach which are particularly profitable. However, there are areas of North Miami that would be less profitable. If you offer a plan in Miami Beach you must offer that same plan in Overtown or Little Havana.

Mr. TOWNS. So that would be, you think, essential that we do the same thing in our health care reform?

Mr. COOK. Absolutely. Absolutely. There should be no redlining, and we worked very hard to prevent that.

Mr. TOWNS. Your testimony indicates that during your initial round of requests for proposals alliances received bids from 46 partnerships offering over 1,000 plans, I think you said.

Mr. COOK. Yes, sir. That is right.

Mr. TOWNS. With that amount of competition, why do you believe alliances need the power to negotiate prices?

Mr. COOK. Well, sir, I think the question is, the hard question is, and excuse me for being a little bit ambivalent here, I am not certain whether you need exclusivity or whether you need negotiation, and I would like to talk to the merits of both.

I have heard a lot of discussion here this morning about the lack of—that people want voluntary competing alliances. What I will tell you is one of the weaknesses of the Florida alliances is the games that are played outside the alliance.

In other words, there is some significant evidence in a number of our alliances that insurance agents are steering poorer risks into alliances instead of out of the alliances, and are being encouraged by their carriers to do so.

And so, with the lack of an exclusive coverage area, in other words, without the ability to cover all employers 1 to 50, and, of course, we as Americans resent any kind of mandate that we are not participating in, with the lack of that then there is always the opportunity for insurance companies and insurance agents to steer bad risks into alliances instead of outside.

Now, the other question is, if you have exclusivity, which was, frankly, the original Jackson Hole model, do you need negotiation? And you probably don't.

If you have exclusivity and choice, you probably don't have to negotiate, as Mr. Wetzell indicated, and, in fact, negotiation may encourage some kind of cost shifting from large employer—or from small employers to large employers if you do.

But without exclusivity or negotiation, then you have the problems of the Florida alliances. We offer a great deal of choice. We were initially able to significantly reduce prices, but over the long haul I am not sure how long we are going to be able to do that if the games, the inside/outside games are allowed to be played.

Mr. WETZELL. If I could comment, Mr. Chair. One of the reasons we got organized, if you think about a big self-insured company, in effect we have been alliances for years. We buy on behalf of all of our employees and retirees and pool their risk.

And what we saw happening in the Twin Cities market is a phenomenon called shadow pricing. When we didn't actively negotiate with the insurance companies, they would look at what the premiums were that were being charged by their competition, and the least cost effective plan with the highest premium and set their rates just below that.

So, if you can't actively negotiate, the savings don't get passed on to the purchaser, and you can't ultimately pass them on to the consumer. Because in our market the insurance industry has done a fairly sophisticated job of figuring out what the competition was pricing their products at and shadow pricing their premiums up to that level, so the efficiencies weren't passed on.

The other piece that we really feel has been ignored and neglected is aggressive purchaser expectations on legitimate quality improvement. It is all focused on premium and risk selection and dollars, and not based on what really goes on day to day inside the doctors office and inside the hospitals on how you can become more efficient.

And that is where we very strongly advocate an active role for alliances, especially to specify very aggressive quality standards to make health plans and providers compete on quality, not just based on their ability to select risk, price off of each other and compete solely on price. The quality piece is critical, in our opinion, more critical than price negotiation in a lot of ways, where we need active authority to negotiate with plans based on quality standards.

Mr. COOK. Mr. Chairman, if I could fill a little bit of that in on that as well. Of course, our plans do aggressively work the quality angle. We are collecting a great deal of data on patient outcome, which we will be providing on comparison sheets.

So, it is not simply—we couldn't agree more with Mr. Wetzell. If you concentrate on quality you will reduce prices. If you concentrate solely on price, you may not improve quality. So quality ought to be the primary concern, and everything we do ought to be driven by our concern for higher quality care.

We also are one of only two States, and we would strongly advocate that the Congress look at mandating accreditation by one of the national accreditation boards. We are one of only two States that require that all of our HMOs be nationally accredited.

Mr. TOWNS. What I would like to do at this time is to yield to Mr. Mica. I do have questions for Mr. Adkins and Mr. Wetzell, but we will come back on a second round—and probably a third round.

Congressman Mica.

Mr. MICA. Thank you, Mr. Chairman. I appreciate your holding this hearing and trying to get some input on the status of what is happening outside the beltway with the successes and failures of alliances.

It's good to see Mr. Cook from Florida, and right off the bat I have a couple of questions for you.

The first one is, Why has Florida gone through all this trouble to come up with a health care reform package while we in Congress are then dealing with the same kinds of questions and may, in fact, come up with our own solutions?

Mr. COOK. Well, sir, we didn't feel that we could wait. Based on some of the struggles you are going through, it looks like it may take you a little while to get there, and our problem is we were experiencing over 20 percent increases in our health care costs and significant problems. We are the fourth—we have the fourth highest uninsured rate in the country, as I was explaining to the chairman earlier. So we didn't feel like we could wait.

We also felt like you all might be able to learn a little bit from our experience. We know that it is a little bit hard to do bottom up, having been top down. We were here for a number of years, as you know, but we felt like you might be able to learn from some of our successes and whatever our failures were.

And we have strengths and weaknesses in our alliances, but we felt like we couldn't wait. We felt like we ought to move ahead, and, you know, relating to Mr. Jefferson, he used to think that folks at the local level might be able to give a little bit of information to folks at the Federal level.

Mr. MICA. Let me ask real quickly about some comparisons between what Florida is doing and has had some limited experience with and, say, what is being proposed by the administration. For example, what about mandatory versus voluntary alliances? Why did Florida take the approach it is taking, and why do you think the States should be permitted that leeway?

Mr. COOK. Well, sir, let's just say we have tremendous respect for what the administration's trying to do. This is, I think, one of the greatest social and economic problems. Health care is the largest industry in our State. It exceeds tourism. Over the last year it is a $40 billion industry. It is tremendously influential in our politics and our economic life. And if you can't form that system you can't improve Florida's economy.

Mr. MICA. Well, do you favor mandatory or voluntary alliances?

Mr. COOK. Well, sir, I think it is wise for a State like Florida to begin with a voluntary alliance. But recognize, as we are beginning to recognize, the problems of the voluntary alliances, which is there is a temptation within a voluntary alliance structure for the existing industry to shift its bad risks to the alliance and to set up different premium structures or rate structures for its insurance agents and brokers so that brokers are paid less to go into the alliance than they are outside of the alliance. There are any number of games that are being played in our voluntary alliances.

So, while we support what we are doing and we are enthusiastic about what we are doing, and we are experiencing some good things, the problem with the voluntary alliance is that there are too many games that are allowed to be played. Now, maybe we can correct those short of making the alliances mandatory. However, we need to recognize we are experiencing some significant problems while we are providing some significant benefits.

Mr. MICA. Are the voluntary alliances becoming sort of the dumping ground for the uninsurable or the difficult to insure?

Mr. COOK. Initially, when we looked at the companies that have come in, and remember, sir, we have actually been providing insurance for a month, so I can't say that our experience is enduring. We saw a lot of bad risk being assumed, companies that had never provided insurance before.

Now, I must say in the last 2 weeks we have seen a blip of larger firms coming in and participating and joining in the alliances. I think in a year or so we might be able to give you more information as to what we are seeing. But we do need to recognize that agents, some of the agents who have embraced the alliance are telling us that there are companies, there are carriers and other agents which are shifting their bad risk to our alliances.

Mr. MICA. The GAO report that I looked through said that the alliance boards have little, if any, employee or consumer representation. What is the situation in Florida?

Mr. COOK. Well, that has not been our experience, sir. As you know, we have 17-member boards. There are three consumer representatives on the board. Each of our appointing officers are able to appoint consumer representatives to the board and actively do that.

I think if we were going to look again at it we might not have such large boards.

Mr. MICA. So, you have 17-member boards.

Mr. COOK. Yes, sir.

Mr. MICA. That was going to be my next question. Have you found that too cumbersome? Maybe you are suffering from over-representation. There are 11 separate boards and there are 17-member boards.

Mr. COOK. That is correct.

Mr. MICA. Are you finding that cumbersome and expensive? Were they initially funded at $275,000?

Mr. COOK. Yes, sir. We provided them with initial funds of $275,000 to begin their operation, rent their equipment and rent their office space, and now they will become self-sufficient, I dare say, within the next year.

It has been a little bit of a challenge, and it has been a challenge for some of the members of the board. And we put a 2-year sunset in our law so that we are going to be able to look at that during the next legislative session, take testimony and try to determine what the boards think is an appropriate structure.

But I don't sense that consumers feel that they are under-represented. In fact, if you look at some of the press clips that we have provided, I think consumers are actually very excited, and this is something that I would say is a very strong part of developing a geographic alliance with unique and exclusive geographic boundaries.

These folks do become representatives of their area. They are voluntary members of the board. They have put in literally hundreds of hours unpaid, and I would stress that, you know, it has always perplexed me a little bit to hear about these huge bureaucracies. Well, we have 11 boards and we have less than 30 employees staffing those 11 boards. Most of that work is done by business people and consumers in a local area, who are doing it because they want to improve the quality and cost of health care in their area.

So, I think you can do it without a major bureaucracy, and you can make it efficient, and the boards can be very effective.

Mr. MICA. One other question. Then I will go back to the chairman and catch you on the next round.

Mr. COOK. Yes, sir.

Mr. MICA. Let's see, you have really only a short period of experience so far. How long do you think it is going to take, or what is the timeframe, before we get some real picture as to the success of this program overall?

Mr. COOK. I happen to think that the alliances can't fail, sir. The only question is how much they succeed.

Most small businesses today are alone with the sharks in the water, and they have no opportunity to do what they are doing here. I just talked with a good friend of mine, a new friend of mine, an agent from Pensacola, who just insured a firm for the first time. It was one of the more exciting experiences, he said, in his professional life. It is a firm with nine employees and they have three different plans.

Now, the idea that a 9-employee firm, a very small business, would be able to have three different plans uniquely tailored, three different carriers providing three different plans uniquely tailored to the individual concerns of consumers and employees in that firm is something that he finds incredibly exciting.

At the same time he was a little bit frustrated to find that one of the firms that he had referred to a large carrier had been baited and switched to a more expensive plan because of the lack of mandatory coverage, so—or lack of exclusivity. So there is some very good news and there are some——

Mr. MICA. Problems.

Mr. COOK. Yes, sir.

Mr. MICA. OK. Well, my time has expired, so I will yield back to the chairman.

Mr. TOWNS. The gentleman is absolutely right, his time has expired.

Let me just sort of raise some questions with you, Mr. Wetzell. How were you able to do both?

Mr. WETZELL. Well, we issued an RFP, Mr. Chairman, and asked for things in the market that we knew weren't out there. One of the things we asked was that the system that we contracted with be able to scientifically document what care was necessary to benefit the patient, what care wasn't, and how they measured quality and outcomes. And what that stimulated was the creation of a nonprofit institution by the contractor that was given our business.

It is governed by purchasers and providers, where the providers sit down and scientifically define with their peers when it is appropriate to do a test, whether it is not appropriate to do a test, when they need to see a patient for a viral condition, for example, when they don't, and then we created incentives with the providers.

If they are able to eliminate waste through these practice parameters that they develop, not the insurance companies, we share the gain 50–50 with them. And then to protect the consumers, which is the ultimate measure of whether or not the society is going to think we are doing the right thing, we have the providers accountable for measuring outcomes and annually measuring patient satisfaction and measuring population health to make sure that the ultimate customer, the individual consumer's needs are being served by this process where the doctors set down in their own governed setting with financial incentives to eliminate waste.

And, if I can take a minute to give you a specific example? The first guideline we had our doctors do was for bladder infection for women, and there are about 5.5 million episodes of bladder infection in this country a year. In a fee-for-service environment through an insurer, even through most HMOs that are discount fee-for-service arrangements, the providers don't get paid for treating a woman for a bladder infection unless they make her come in for an office visit.

When we set up an incentive program where you didn't necessarily have to see the patient to get paid for taking care of their health need, what the doctors came up with was a method where they can screen 70 percent of the women out that don't even need to see a doctor to get treated for bladder infection. All they need is an antibiotic. So we cut the cost of treating a bladder infection by half, eliminated the inconvenience for the patient of an unnecessary office visit, saved that patient their copayment. So it is better service. It is quicker service. And it saves money.

And the other thing we found is that doctors were routinely overprescribing antibiotics, and this is in a managed care community that has a reputation for high quality. And when you do that that leads—it gets rid of the bladder infection but leads to a different kind of infection, a yeast infection, which drives up cost and isn't good quality. And we found 185 different ways just in this one example where bladder infections were being treated in 20 different medical groups. That is what is driving cost.

Mr. TOWNS. In your experience, how can we prevent insurance companies from redlining certain populations?

Mr. WETZELL. Well, for the self-insured market it is not an issue because we cover all of our folks regardless of what part of the community they live in, so self-insured companies don't redline. It is more for the insured business.

Our feeling is that when these health plans bid for alliance business the regulatory process should define a geographic region that they have to serve, and we have seen evidence of that in the Twin Cities where there is a lot of managed care. What the health plans do to avoid high risk is they just quote premiums or fee schedules to doctors that serve high-risk populations that the doctors won't accept. So, they don't get into the network.

They don't have a contract. And those underserved communities don't have access to providers in their community, and that is how the plans avoid serving them.

So, you just set a rule that says you have to have a network of providers, if it is a managed care plan, that covers the entire community.

Mr. TOWNS. Let me raise this question with you, Mr. Adkins. How big a problem is geographic redlining by the insurance industry?

Mr. ADKINS. Well, by the industry at large, I think it is a serious problem. As you know, the property and casualty industry is undergoing some substantial scrutiny by the States, and there are bills under consideration by the Federal Government, to look at this matter.

On the health side, it has been a continual problem as companies selected out the better risks and try to miss everybody else. That could still be a problem in the alliance structure.

And, as Mr. Wetzell has said, if you deal with the geography through a Federal standard, I think you can address that issue. SMSA seems most appropriate. I think the Florida model is a good one in terms of the way they have structured their alliances, although maybe they have too many. I am not sure what the answer is on that front.

But certainly in terms of rating as well as geography, it needs to be as broad as possible to allow—to encourage the largest number of people to be incorporated into that subset and prevent the smaller subdivisions which effectively allow a separating out of the lower income and the upper income, the healthier and the less healthy.

Mr. TOWNS. Can you expand more fully on the 1993 study by the Center for Health Care Rights in Los Angeles regarding the problems of Medicare enrollees?

Mr. ADKINS. Yes. As you know, there is a whole debate about what kind of outcomes are achieved based on different kinds of reimbursement mechanisms, whether it is a fee-for-schedule or capitated rate, and there have been a number of studies, including that referenced by the Center for Health Care Rights, which have looked to evaluate the differences.

I think the debate has come up with some very substantial conclusions. That, in fact, there are differences in the kinds of health care treatments and outcomes based on reimbursement mechanisms.

One of the things we would like to see the alliance system do, and we do support Federal standards as Mr. Wetzell does, not just the State standards, to establish a minimum floor. One of the things we would like to see the States do is make sure that the quality assurance measures are tracked; that is, diagnoses, treatments, outcomes, and other indices of quality, that those are tracked by reimbursement mechanism, so that a real distinction can be made based on each kind of reimbursement system.

We think that will go a long way toward not only educating the policymakers and regulators about quality care and how you maintain quality, but will allow consumers to judge and make a decision as to what kind of benefit they want depending on the kinds of treatments they anticipate.

Mr. TOWNS. Last question before I yield back. What are some of the unique concerns for senior citizens regarding alliances within a managed competition system? Mr. Adkins?

Mr. ADKINS. I am not sure I can speak to that in particular, although there are obvious coverage issues that relate to overlapping benefits and there needs to be some coordination of benefits to address that matter. Seniors tend to have more substantial health needs. They tend to have mobility issues that other populations don't? Their medical needs tend to be greater. Their pharmaceutical consumption is higher, et cetera. And one of the things we would like to see in terms of a rating classification limitation is that the bands for consideration of age be limited.

Let me reference the NAIC. They have now got age bands of 5 years and no real cap in terms of differential between the lowest premium and the highest premium that can be offered. This is a very serious problem, and we think the NAIC is erring. And we hate to see the States proceed in that manner.

The Federal Government should establish, we believe, at minimum 10-year age bands as well as a differential, a maximum of 1 to 3, so that the highest premium is no more than three times the lowest premium. And we think that will increase accessibility. to that vulnerable population.

Mr. COOK. Mr. Chairman, we would like to comment on that as well.

Mr. TOWNS. You have a State that has a lot of senior citizens, right?

Mr. COOK. Yes, sir, we do, and as you know, having visited south Florida recently. We couldn't agree more with Mr. Adkins. We moved to a modified community rating standard which still allowed folks to use insurance companies to use age as a proxy or a risk-adjusting mechanism. We think that the 5-year age bands are very inadequate and potentially extremely unfair.

The problem, of course, we have in moving to a pure community rating standard is that if the Congress can't get its mind around universal coverage it is very difficult to narrow the age bands or make other risk adjustments. In other words, if we can't ensure that the young invulnerables get into the system and pay while they are young and invulnerable, then it is very difficult for us to appropriately price older, sicker people in this market.

And that is part of our problem with universal coverage. We don't seem to be willing to bite that bullet at this moment right now. And unless we can bring younger, healthier people who are less likely to insure themselves into this, then it is very difficult to make the appropriate adjustments we should for age and keep insurance affordable for older people. And, of course, that is a major concern for us in Florida.

Mr. TOWNS. Thank you very much.

At this time I yield to Congressman Mica.

Mr. MICA. One of my major concerns, gentlemen, has been waste, fraud and abuse in the current system, particularly the Medicaid system. Through the leadership of our chairman we have pursued Medicaid fraud in an unrelenting fashion, particularly in the State of Florida. I believe it was August 2 or 3 of last year, in the hearing that the chairman organized in New York City, GAO came forward with a report that disclosed an incredible amount of waste, fraud and abuse in the Medicaid system, Medicaid, pill mills and other health care things.

Unfortunately, one of the worst offenders was Florida. We have since gotten the legislature to move the Medicaid fraud unit from a State auditor's function to the Attorney General's office.

The Department of Justice has now made this more of a priority at the national level. We have got 10 additional FBI agents, a Hispanic speaking investigator and the legislature is also appropriating more funds to go after that.

This is a huge rip off. I was just handed a press release from the Department of Justice that says the Department has announced a record fine of $33 million or something against one psychiatric care provider. These are mindboggling amounts that the system gets ripped off for.

I preface my question with those remarks and ask you this: what are your alliances doing to ensure that some of this waste, fraud and abuse that we have seen in the past doesn't spill over to some of the new programs and activities such as you are involved in.

Mr. COOK. Well, sir, first of all, let me compliment you and the chairman for your leadership here. This has been a significant problem for us. We have raised this issue a number of times, as you know, in Florida.

Part of our problem is like many other States the enforcement function was spread throughout us. The Agency for Health Care Administration houses a Medicaid fraud and abuse unit. However, enforcement of that function ultimately, we were highlighting cases and bringing cases up but then getting the Auditor General to do what he needed to do and ultimately the Attorney General to do what he needed to do is a bit problematic.

I think this is an appropriate area for Congress to look very hard at. I think your leadership has helped us in Florida get a better handle on this, and we appreciate that. But it is a significant problem. That Congress needs to look at how States employ the enforcement function.

Florida is probably not unlike many other States where the enforcement is spread out throughout the bureaucracy without clear lines of authority in some cases and accountability in some cases, and unless those clear lines of accountability and enforcement are there you can't do it.

Second, it is another problem of universal coverage. The confusing maze of insurance benefits and providers and third-party payers makes it very, very difficult to establish standards, enforce standards, and follow through when you know and see abuse.

In our particular State, I handle the licensing of quality enforcement for health care facilities. The Department of Professional Regulation does the licensing and quality enforcement of physicians and professionals. Until your hearing and the movement by the legislature, the auditor general handle up on fraud and abuse. And you can't do that.

But again, without universal coverage, without a clean line of authority leading up to the Department of Justice for Federal funds, it is very, very difficult to do the kinds of things we need to do. Too often, we know exactly where the abusing parties are, but getting a handle on them is very difficult to do.

Mr. MICA. Are you putting into place any mechanism to monitor these activities? Now, we have dozens of plans and lot more participants. I know competition will help, you know, drive the price, but is there somebody guarding the henhouse, so to speak?

Mr. COOK. Well, I think it kind of comes back to Mr. Wetzell's remarks and Mr. Adkins' remarks on quality, which we couldn't agree with and endorse more. If quality is a preeminent concern of the health care system, then price and honesty in the system and the ethics of the system will inevitably improve. The problem you often have is if price becomes the sole concern of the system, then other things, other problems languish. So, we would argue for a very strong quality enforcement.

Again, we would argue for some clear line of authority in universal coverage. We believe that as long as there is significant gaps in the system and too many payers paying too many different people it is very difficult to enforce.

We also believe in very strong Federal regulation to hold the States accountable for Federal moneys, and for enforcing fraud and abuse complaints. You know, we would endorse anything that this committee would come up with. The Governor feels very, very strongly that that lack of a clear Federal voice is a problem.

Further, I think we need to recognize that what your hearing pointed out was not only significant problems in Medicaid but in Medicare. The fact, and this is kind of the real problem you have when there is a lack of local participation. A federally, a strict federally run program with no State participation or enforcement.

Medicare is the biggest payer in our State. Yet, we have nothing to say about quality in Medicare. I receive literally hundreds of letters from seniors who feel that they are being abused in the Medicare system. Yet, I have no ability, other than to refer their letters somewhere else, to enforce their quality complaints.

States should be responsible for any payer and every payer in their State, the private payers, the public payers and the Federal payers in that case, and we need to look at clear lines of authority there and clear lines of partnership between the Federal and State Government.

Mr. MICA. I think it would be good, Mr. Cook, based on your experience again, to recommend to the committee, maybe you could in writing, some areas where we could look at this and possibly recommend some improvements, because it is a major area of concern, and, you know, folks are getting ripped off, not getting their money's worth.

Mr. COOK. Absolutely.

Mr. MICA. And then the closer you get to that particular service the people know where the abuse is or where they are not getting the attention, or the taxpayer getting their dollars' worth. So, we have worked in our own way in trying to improve the Medicaid and some of those services. Maybe you could help us in that regard and provide that, maybe a little commentary.

And, if the chairman will let me continue, I have a couple more questions.

Mr. WETZELL. Mr. Mica, if I might add just a brief comment?

Mr. MICA. Yes.

Mr. WETZELL. Medicare-Medicaid fraud in our view is largely driven by the financial incentives instead of by the reimbursement policies. When you work in an industry where you are awarded based on how many units you can bill for the incentive is towards fraudulent behavior based on units of services that may or may not have been delivered much less whether or not they benefit the patient.

So, we believe the issue is how the industry is structured and what the financial incentives are, and our belief is you need to integrate hospitals, doctors, psychiatric services into systems that are accountable for managing the health of their enrollees. And you negotiate arrangements where they are held accountable on their per member per month expense. The better they manage the health of that group, the lower their cost and the more profit they make versus how many units they deliver.

So, we believe that prepayment, the integrated systems that are held accountable with very specific quality measures that could protect the consumers will eliminate a lot of the need for the State or the Federal Government to do all that inspection, because all the incentives are aligned toward keeping people healthy and not wasting money as opposed to billing for services which may or may not benefit the patient.

Mr. MICA. That leads me to another question, and I am concerned about the quality, you know, the price, the ripping off of the—most of the alliances, though, are geared to people who really are employed, you know, small employers, which is good. There has been a big gap there.

But what do we see as far as low income or unemployed? How are alliances addressing service access and availability of coverage for folks like that?

Mr. COOK. I think that is an excellent question, sir, and it is a very, very complex one. And I don't know that we have an adequate answer.

But we have begun to develop an answer, because the problem we have is that we estimate probably 500,000 or the uninsured people we have in our State, maybe 600,000 of the uninsured people we have in our State live below 100 percent of the poverty level, and are part-time employees in many cases. Most of them have jobs at different times of the year, but they don't have necessarily a steady employer. In some cases they might be migrant workers. In some cases they might have small businesses. In some cases they might be self-employed.

One of the things that we have begun this year and will hopefully be able to pass if we can ever get our health care reform bill passed in this even numbered year is the idea of working with large public systems, what we are calling community health partnerships. And these large public systems in the past have been providing care to the uninsured.

As we move toward insuring more and more people, and, of course, as you know, in Florida we have a major initiative to insure about a million people this year. With the decrease in that burden, we think that these community health partnerships, and in particular we are talking about Jackson Memorial Hospital in Miami, the North and South Broward Hospital Districts in Fort Lauderdale, the Palm Beach Health Care District in Palm Beach, Tampa General Hospital, and a number of the public providers in Tampa are forming partnerships because the fact of the matter is under 150 percent of the poverty level with many part-time employees one needs to work harder to ensure people don't use the emergency room as their primary form of access even if they are insured.

Mr. MICA. Right. You end up with the most expensive, least effective, poorest quality care.

Mr. COOK. Absolutely. But we have two or three areas that are really concentrating on bringing those people in and watching their emergency room usage drop substantially. But that means following up. Providing social services, overlay social services along with health care services.

Mr. MICA. Well, there are a number elements to the current system that really concern me, and one is something you described. As you force people, really, almost into welfare and poverty with no other alternative and then they either lie or cheat or not disclose their assets or something to get care, where they could be willing participants if they had some opportunity according to their ability, if they are part-time workers, to contribute to it, and then they end up with the worst possible care.

Whereas, if Medicaid, which they end up on, was converted to the private sector where they were able to contribute, if they only work part-time, and maybe $5 a week or $10 a week, you would have some revenue source. You would also encourage people to work and not rely only on waiting till the critical thing and then going for Medicaid or hiding their assets.

Mr. COOK. Well, in fact, Mr. Mica, what you have just described in the true sense that great minds think alike is the Governor's health care plan where he wants to use Medicaid savings to provide private health insurance and allow people under 100 percent of the poverty level to pay some small portion of that so that they can purchase private health insurance. And if you can encourage other members of our legislature to come aboard, we can pass that thing and get on with it.

Mr. MICA. I have done that. And that really was my last point. That the legislature did shoot down some of these reform proposals.

But I think that it is important to fill that missing gap. The alliances which you all are doing is a good beginning, but you still have a lot of folks out there that aren't covered that have fallen through the cracks, that are getting the worst care, that are being forced into poverty that are willing to even pay and willing to even work some and contribute, and they are all being discouraged by the current system.

Mr. COOK. Well, we agree with you completely, sir. I happen to think that the best—as you know, I was budget director of our State during a difficult period and I will tell you that the best welfare reform is health care reform, if we can provide that security. Many people would gladly leave a welfare dependency status if they could provide health care to them and their families, some small children.

Mr. MICA. Mr. Chairman, thank you.

Mr. TOWNS. Thank you.

Let me say to all the witnesses I really appreciate your testimony and I think you have been extremely helpful in many, many ways.

Also, Mr. Cook, I would like to thank you for the kind words in terms of the work on behalf of this committee. I am certain that the members will be happy to hear that and to read it, of course.

The other thing I would like to just say, though, as I look at this whole process, though I am hoping that as we move, and I think that Florida is moving and I am happy to see it, and that maybe you are right. Maybe that as a result of what you are doing, maybe eventually we will get going up here. As you know, we have not gotten too far. But we are still optimistic in a lot of ways.

But I think you are right that it has to be done at this level in order to really, really make it work.

Mr. COOK. Yes, sir.

Mr. TOWNS. Because we do not want people moving from one State to another because of the fact that certain services are in one State and you can't get them in another one. I think we have to do it here to make certain that it is done and done properly.

Mr. COOK. Absolutely.

Mr. TOWNS. So we welcome your comments in that regard, and believe me, we will look very closely and carefully at that. My closing statement, we have heard persuasive testimony that voluntary alliances are working. If carefully designed, voluntary alliances can make health care affordable for millions of Americans. However, there are problems.

Alliances need sufficient authority to negotiate price. They need incentives to provide affordable and quality health care. Alliance boards must better reflect the demographics of their communities. Insurance companies and alliances must not be allowed to redline certain communities.

We must also provide for adequate grievance procedures to protect consumers and senior citizens. I intend to take these and other recommendations we have heard today to our colleagues in the Congress. As we move into the final phase of health care reform, I think it is important that we take all these factors under consideration.

Fraud and abuse, very, very important. And I think we have to be concerned about fraud and abuse as to how it moves, because the problem that we see today could be different tomorrow. As you know, today we see overbilling. That people are billing and are

138

charging for things that they have not done, and this is a classic example here in terms of this information that we just received.

But also, we have to be concerned about the fact that people need, and as a result of not getting in order to keep down costs we have to be concerned about that as well. So as we move to health care reform, then we have to look at the fact that—and I think you said it so well, and I want to let you know I plan to use that sometimes, where you said take two aspirins and call us when you are rich. I will be using that. And the first time I will give you credit for it, Mr. Cook, but after that it will be mine.

Mr. COOK. Sir, you don't have to give me credit for anything. Use it yourself.

Mr. TOWNS. So thank you very much for your testimony.

This committee hearing is concluded.

[Whereupon, at 11:45 a.m., the subcommittee was adjourned.]

O